THE REAL JESUS

The Misguided Quest for the Historical Jesus
and the Truth of the Traditional Gospels

LUKE TIMOTHY JOHNSON

HarperSanFrancisco
An Imprint of HarperCollinsPublishers

THE REAL JESUS: *The Misguided Quest for the Historical Jesus and the Truth of the Traditional Gospels.* Copyright © 1996 by Luke Timothy Johnson. All rights reserved. Printed in the United States of America. No part of this book may be used or reproduced in any manner whatsoever without written permission except in the case of brief quotations embodied in critical articles and reviews. For information address HarperCollins Publishers, 10 East 53rd Street, New York, NY 10022.

HarperCollins Web Site: http://www.harpercollins.com

HarperCollins®, ♨®, and HarperSanFrancisco™
are trademarks of HarperCollins Publishers Inc.

FIRST HARPERCOLLINS PAPERBACK EDITION PUBLISHED IN 1997

Library of Congress Cataloging-in-Publication Data
Johnson, Luke Timothy.
The real Jesus / Luke Timothy Johnson. — 1st ed.
Includes bibliographical references and index.
ISBN 0–06–064177–0 (cloth)
ISBN 0–06–064166–5 (pbk.)
1. Jesus Christ—Biography—History and criticism.   2. Jesus
Christ—Historicity.   3. Jesus Christ—History of doctrines—
20th century.   4. Jesus Seminar.   5. Funk, Robert Walter.
I. Title.
BT301.9.J64   1996   95–19885
232'.09'045—dc20

99 00 ❖ HAD 10 9

Luke Timothy Johnson's *The Real Jesus*

"In the best of the recent flow of books [on Jesus] . . . Johnson offers a devastating critique of those scholars who prefer their own reconstructed Jesus to the one attested in the New Testament."

—*Newsweek*

"Johnson . . . is at the center of the newest round in what has been called the Jesus Wars."

—Peter Steinfels, *New York Times*

"*The Real Jesus* already has marked [Johnson] . . . as one of the sharpest critics of the field."

—*U.S. News & World Report*

"More than simply being a critique of the historical Jesus enterprise, Johnson's book provides a positive statement about what it means to have a genuine, contemporary faith in the living Jesus."

—*Philadelphia Inquirer*

"Johnson has mounted a frontal assault that demolishes the pretensions of the Jesus Seminar and reaffirms the Christ of faith. . . . *The Real Jesus* is one of the most exhilarating religious books published in this decade."

—*Christianity Today*

"Finally, a passionately argued but fair response to the Jesus Seminar from an established scholar. . . . Highly recommended."

—*Library Journal*

"Johnson exposes the Jesus Seminar for what it is: self-promotion resting on tendentious scholarship. This book is a clarion call for a hard look at much of contemporary biblical scholarship. Provocative and clear-headed polemics—a must read."

—Lawrence S. Cunningham, professor of theology,
University of Notre Dame

"Johnson effectively and deliciously skewers a lot of half-baked scholarship. But there is more: Johnson is challenging everyone who is seriously interested in the Christian story to rethink . . . faith's connection with history."

—Wayne A. Meeks, author of *The Origin of Christian Morality*
and general editor of *The HarperCollins Study Bible*

"Take a seasoned and serious scholar, who has read everything he should and thought hard about it. Point him at the hottest issue of the day. Insist that every sentence possess scholarly rigor and popular clarity. What do you get? Luke Johnson's *The Real Jesus*. This book exposes, by example as well as argument, the shallowness of much would-be scholarship about Jesus and the pretensions of much would-be popularization. The intellectual power of this book presents a challenge to unthinking piety; its deep Christian devotion, with no loss of scholarly precision, challenges unthinking reductionism, not least that of the 'Jesus Seminar.'"

—N. T. Wright, author of *The New Testament and the People of God*

"This timely book offers an engaging account of what serious historical scholarship can—and cannot—say about the Jesus of history. Johnson refocuses the debate by posing fundamental questions about the relation between history, tradition, and faith."

—Richard B. Hays, professor of New Testament, Duke Divinity School;
author of *The Moral Vision of the New Testament*

"The Jesus of cheap scholarship, the Jesus-as-I-personally-like-to-imagine-him, has been zealously promoted through the past decade like a fizzy new drink. Thank goodness, then, for a cool, clear glass of sober scholarship from Luke Johnson."

—Dr. James D. G. Dunn, Lightfoot Professor of Divinity, University of Durham

"Hurrah! At a time when confusion abounds about who the 'real Jesus' is, Johnson sounds a clarion note: The 'real Jesus' is not the reconstructed Jesus of a scholarship become unself-critical, but the Jesus who confronts persons in the texts of the New Testament as the resurrected Lord. A welcome guide to the contemporary discussion of the quest for the historical Jesus!"

—Jack Dean Kingsbury, Aubrey Lee Brooks Professor of Biblical Theology, Union
Theological Seminary in Virginia; editor of *Interpretation: A Journal of Bible
and Theology*

"A powerful and learned challenge to the deluge of recent works that claim to offer 'the real Jesus.'"

—John R. Donahue, S.J., professor of New Testament, Graduate Theological
Union and Jesuit School of Theology, Berkeley

"A devastating attack on the claims of the 'Jesus Seminar' and other revisionist lives of Jesus, this book challenges the whole enterprise of writing 'lives of Jesus.' Christian faith has never been based on the historical Jesus. It reflects communal experience of the living, risen Lord."

—Pheme Perkins, professor of theology, Boston College

"Luke Johnson offers a provocative assessment . . . sure to evoke sharp response."

—Abraham J. Malherbe, Buckingham Professor Emeritus of New Testament Criticism
and Interpretation, Yale Divinity School

"Johnson's book is a breath of fresh air. . . . Johnson restores the proper meaning of the 'real Jesus.'"

—Joseph A. Fitzmyer, S.J., professor emeritus of biblical studies,
Catholic University of America

THE REAL JESUS

Contents

I wrote this book to blow the whistle on a form of scholarship I consider misguided and misleading. The results have been both surprising and, on reflection, predictable.

Those whose work I have challenged have not faltered for a moment in their pursuits. If anything, sales of the books I criticized have gone up rather than down. By the time *The Real Jesus* appears in paperback, Robert Funk will have published *Honest to Jesus* (HarperSanFrancisco, 1996), another work advancing the goals of the Jesus Seminar, and the seminar itself is producing its conclusions concerning the deeds of Jesus. Professors Borg and Crossan continue to write and lecture without any significant modification of their views or their methods. Indeed, their mega–media event "Jesus at 2000" might be taken as the apex of their efforts and the dissemination of their views.

Worse still, from my perspective, the sound of my whistle has been caught up into the surrounding noise and orchestrated as part of a continuing media event. This has been hard for me to take. I understand it, but I do not like it. The effect of my book's publication on the media was apparently to change a ten-year series of "dog bites man" stories into a "man bites dog" story. By agreeing to take part in an e-mail debate with professors Borg and Crossan coordinated by Harper San Francisco after the "Jesus at 2000" event—a debate that yielded little insight but confirmed the distance between the participants on the most important points—I found myself caught up in the media event of Easter 1996: three newsweekly magazines (*Time, Newsweek, U.S. News & World Report*) had Jesus on their covers, and their cover stories made what should be a serious scholarly discussion look more like a "debate." This newsweekly attention, in turn, generated radio and television interviews and a further television "debate" (on Trinity Church Broadcasting, May 1, 1996), this one joined by professors Deirdre Good and N. T. Wright.

In short, the very pattern identified in chapters 2 and 3 of this book was enacted. Starting as a critic of the way in which an important subject had been routed through the media rather than through the church and the academy, I found myself co-opted by the same process, with the points in my argument increasingly reduced to the level of comments on personalities, or position-taking sound bites. I was thoroughly hoisted by my own petard. No one is more acutely aware of the irony, and no one left with more of a sense of chagrin, than I.

I cannot complain about the actual coverage by the media. If anything, the attention paid to my book was positive and that given to my argument approving. But I was confirmed in my sense that the media is the wrong place for such discussions to occur, not only because of its inability to deal with substantive issues adequately, but because participation in the media's productions inevitably draws people away from their primary cultural involvements. The power of the media to entice participation in its own efforts is powerful, for who can resist the chance to appear as worthy of attention by the priests of the culture? Also strong is the media's capacity to intrude into and disrupt one's life. In my case, I cannot remember a semester when I felt more strongly that my students were not receiving my best efforts. Once again, I found myself ironically guilty of the criticism I make in chapter 3, that those who seek to influence public opinion do so at risk to the more fundamental and important transformation of minds by teaching.

If I have not contributed significantly to the cessation of bad historical scholarship, do I have any sense of accomplishment? Yes, on several fronts. First, I have been pleased that many other scholars have greeted the book positively. The remarkable prepublication sale of two hundred-plus copies at the Society of Biblical Literature meeting last November suggested that many in the guild had longed for an explicit articulation of a view that they themselves had not been able or had not chosen to make. I am pleased that many of them have read the book, knowing that the ideas here will also find their way to many students for rigorous discussion and analysis in the appropriate setting, that of the classroom. I have received many personal communications from teachers and pastors who are glad to have this alternative position available to their students or parishioners.

Second, a number of scholarly reviews, while not uncritical, have also affirmed and underscored the basic argument of the book. My favorite review was written by Professor Robert Wilken for *Commonweal*. Wilken sees clearly that the book is fundamentally not about the Jesus Seminar but about the much more troubling problem of which the Jesus Seminar is only the most irritating and noisy manifestation, namely, the state of biblical scholarship in the present generation. The ways in which the historical-critical method have run amok are not disconnected from the ways in which biblical scholarship has become detached from communities for whom the writings of the Old and New Testaments have existential and normative importance.

Third, although I am disappointed that the term *historical* is still bandied about without much reflection on its many possible meanings, and remain puzzled by the fact that those pursuing "the historical Jesus" take so little note of the earlier history of this very quest or show so little sense of being instructed by it, I am pleased that this book has helped direct attention to the pivotal character of the resurrection, not simply as one more event in the Jesus story, but as the essential and defining experience from whose perspective Jesus must be understood. By insisting that the resurrection is *not* "historical" (according to my definition) but is, of all things about Jesus, most "real," I have helped shift the conversation, at least within the church, from the reconstruction of a figure of the past to a response to a living person in the present. The Archdiocese of Portland, for example, is planning an extensive series of lectures and workshops for its clergy and laity, which will not simply consider the current controversy over the historical Jesus, but will take up in a more fundamental way the rich experience of and engagement with the figure of the Christ within the life of the church.

Finally, I have found that the position adopted in this book is not only more "traditional" (as the media would have it) than the positions advanced by the books I criticize, but is also more "radical" than the positions occupied by such scholars as Richard Hays and N. T. Wright. Both of these scholars have applauded aspects of my response to the Seminar and its associates, but they have worried over what they consider to be, first, my skepticism concerning the possibilities of doing real history with Jesus and, second, my emphasis on the resurrection as something more than historical and something more shocking than a simple validation of what Jesus was saying and doing all along.

Although I do not intend to spend the rest of my days in this particular conversation, I should like to state that I find as much to fault with the premise that one can read history directly off the pages of the Gospels as I do with the premise that one must junk the Gospels in order to do history. I worry as much about an interpretation of the resurrection that moves in the direction of resuscitation (in order to keep it "historical") as I do about an interpretation of the resurrection as a psychological adjustment (in order to keep it "historical"). I am as little impressed by the argument that Christianity must be based on a reconstruction of Jesus' eschatological politics as by the position that Christianity should be based on a reconstruction of Jesus' egalitarian politics. The issue is not at all, as these scholars on either side of me want to insist, the legitimacy of doing historical research on the human figure of Jesus. That legitimacy is clearly affirmed by this book. The issue is, rather, the limits of historical reconstruction, and its appropriateness or adequacy for the grounding of Christian faith. If critics to the left and right of me, who themselves hold wildly divergent views of the human person Jesus, all supposedly based on sound historical methodology, complain that my understanding of Jesus is too little historical, and the main reason they adduce is the loss to *faith* for one holding my position, then perhaps the argument of this book that precisely the relationship of history to faith needs careful questioning is not without point.

Luke Timothy Johnson
May 20, 1996
Candler School of Theology
Emory University

Like most teachers and scholars, I much prefer the daily round of the academy—lectures to students, research in the library, writing and reviewing books—to the public forum of celebrity and controversy. And like most teachers and scholars, I have made certain assumptions about this quiet life: that the appropriate way for teachers to exercise power in society is by teaching their students, for example, and that the processes of peer review assure that good scholarship drives out the bad.

Recent events have caused me to reevaluate those assumptions and to write this book. The starting point for my change of mind is where this book starts: the commotion made in the media by the seriously self-advertising Jesus Seminar. I had not paid much attention to its first fulminations. But I was asked over the past few years to review a series of Historical Jesus books, and finally the volume that culminated the Jesus Seminar's first efforts, *The Five Gospels: The Search for the Authentic Words of Jesus*. My reviews of these works were as dismissive as I could make them, since I regarded the books as representing a kind of second-rate scholarship.

It was only when my review of Bishop Spong's *Born of a Woman* in the *Christian Century* stimulated a flood of outraged letters from readers who considered Spong to be an intellectual hero of the faith, and who considered me to be an alienated academic with no interest in the real Jesus, that I was forced to recognize that something serious was going on culturally. I realized for the first time that this sort of ersatz scholarship was being taken for the real thing and that, more startling, the sort of stuff being purveyed by Spong was actually being accepted as the purest gospel by those who called themselves Christian.

This made me look more closely at the Jesus Seminar phenomenon as a symptom of a deeper and more disturbing institutional collapse: the effort by scholars to bypass the ordinary contexts of their activity in order to effect cultural change by direct competition with conservative Christians; the ambiguous role of the media as the arena for this cultural battle; and most of all, the battle over identity boundaries within Christianity itself. At one level, then, this book seeks to sort out some of the strands in a moment of complex cultural confusion.

At another level, this book tries to examine a more fundamental conceptual confusion that long precedes the present controversy, namely, the connection between history and faith. I have not tried to trace with any completeness the development of this discussion as it was carried on by earlier and greater scholars, although I allude at points to certain moments in the debate that I consider important. Instead, I have tried to get at the central issue by analyzing current tendencies in the historical study of the New Testament and Christian origins.

Although my views in this book are outspoken, I hope that my language is courteous. With the exception of John Meier, I do not know personally any of the writers whom I challenge—although after the manuscript was written, I had a good and collegial exchange with John Dominic Crossan in a conversation orchestrated by Gustav Niebuhr, religion reporter for the *New York Times*. I cannot judge their motives or their intentions, except as these have been made available either through their publications or through quotations in the press. I do regard the issues touched on in this book as extremely serious, and worthy of controversy. Much is at stake. If my analysis is correct, the state of biblical scholarship within the church is in critical condition. I do not provide solutions, but I seek to alert others to what I consider serious symptoms. I engage these issues as a scholar fervently dedicated to the free and critical use of the intelligence, as well as a person who would like to be considered worthy of the name of Christian. My deep hope is that such a place is still possible to occupy.

A book that attempts to cover a wide range of difficult issues in fairly clear language and within limited space invites criticism of several kinds. That is fair enough, since I have not refrained from criticism myself in these pages. I know in particular that I have put more balls in the air than I have been able to juggle elegantly. But I am convinced that all these balls need to be put into play. I hope someone else can take them and perform more smoothly.

When I was a Ph.D. student in New Testament studies at Yale University in 1972, I wrote a paper for Professor Wayne Meeks on the Quest of the

Historical Jesus. Meeks thought it mediocre and commented on the cover sheet that I seemed strangely detached from the issue, as though it were not my problem. As a Roman Catholic and (at that time) as a monk in the Benedictine tradition, I agreed: I did not think the historical Jesus was a problem for me or for my tradition. I thought then that this was a peculiarly Protestant problem. Well, Professor Meeks, here is the second draft.

I am blessed with colleagues and students who contribute to everything I write. For this project in particular, I thank for their contributions Carl Holladay, Richard Hays, Steven Kraftchick, William Kurz, William Shepherd, Kyle Keefer, Todd Penner, and above all, Mary Foskett, whose research assistance was invaluable. I appreciate the opportunity to have run some of these ideas through a first rehearsal in reviews for the *Philadelphia Inquirer,* the *Christian Century* (with thanks to David Heim), and *Commonweal* (with thanks to Paul Baumann). Finally, thanks to the wonderfully responsive classes of undergraduates at Indiana University and Emory University, who thought that this approach to the memory of Jesus in the church was worthwhile.

Luke Timothy Johnson
January 3, 1995
Candler School of Theology
Emory University

CHAPTER 1

The Good News and the Nightly News

Recent years have been very good for the Jesus business in America. I don't mean the Jesus business that goes on in churches, but the profitable trade in Jesus by a variety of publications that by creating a commotion in both the academy and the church also create a media-fed demand for more of the same. Sales in scandal are high, stocks in shock are rising, and futures on the historical Jesus are sound. Commerce in the Christ has rarely been better.

In this bullish market, the most remarkable entrepreneurship has been demonstrated by the Jesus Seminar, a ten-year exercise in academic self-promotion that has succeeded in drawing an extraordinary amount of attention to itself. Indeed, it has come to symbolize, for better or worse, the controversy over "the Historical Jesus." Although it stands as a far better example of media manipulation than of serious scholarship, the Jesus Seminar provides the appropriate starting point for considering the character of the present debate over the Historical Jesus as a moment in a culture war in which the institutions of academy, church, and media are drawn into confused conflict and collusion.

The Jesus Seminar

What is the Jesus Seminar? It is a small, self-selected association of academics who meet twice a year to debate the Historical Jesus. The seminar was founded in 1985 by Robert Funk under the auspices of his Westar Institute in Sonoma, California. The Jesus Seminar has been co-chaired from the beginning by John Dominic Crossan of DePaul University in Chicago. It is Funk, however, who has been the most visible and vocal presence for the public, and the shaper of the Seminar's agenda.

Funk is no stranger to entrepreneurship or controversy. A New Testament scholar of well-established credentials, he is the former executive secretary of the Society of Biblical Literature (SBL), the most comprehensive and important learned society for biblical studies. Under his leadership, the SBL grew in size and ambition, linking up with the American Academy of Religion to form a megasociety whose national meeting gathers thousands of scholars from around the world, and spawning a number of publishing ventures under the sponsorship of the Scholars Press. Funk is, in short, a scholar with broad horizons and a knack for power that is highly personalized. Scholars Press, for example, was created by Robert Funk and followed him from his academic appointment in Missoula, Montana, to Chico, California. His directorship of the Scholars Press, however, came to "an abrupt end" with considerable controversy in 1980 (*Council on the Study of Religion Bulletin*, Dec. 1981, p. 143).

The Jesus Seminar is not affiliated with either the Society of Biblical Literature or the other international association for New Testament scholars, the Studiorum Novi Testamenti Societas. It does not, therefore, represent anything like a consensus view of scholars working in the New Testament, but only the views of a group that has been—for all its protestations of diversity—self-selected on the basis of a prior agreement concerning the appropriate goals and methods for studying the Gospels and the figure of Jesus. It is, from beginning to end, an entrepreneurial venture guided by Robert Funk.

These observations do not detract from the legitimacy of the Seminar or its right to conduct its business as it chooses. But in the light of its own statements and media coverage, it is appropriate to clarify its precise academic standing. Sometimes, for example, the phrase "some two hundred scholars" has occurred. To someone unacquainted with the immensity and complexity of higher education in America, two hundred scholars may seem an impressively large number. In fact, however, it is a very small number when placed against the number of New Testament scholars alone who are involved in the work of the SBL (at least half of the 6,900 members of that organization), let alone the thousands more with substantial scholarly training in the New Testament who for personal or ideological reasons do not take part in the society's activities. And even the number *two hundred* is somewhat misleading, since it includes all those who were part of the Seminar's proceedings in any fashion—by receiving its mailings, for example, or reading its reports. A truer estimate of the number of participants who met regularly, wrote papers, and voted on decisions is closer to forty. The Seminar's climactic publication, *The Five Gospels* (to be discussed below), lists seventy-four "fellows" of the seminar. The numbers alone suggest that any claim to represent "scholarship" or the "academy" is ludicrous.

While the Seminar can count among its members some scholars of notable reputation (Funk and Crossan have both produced significant and well-recognized work), and while the Seminar's work increased the visibility of some others (notably Marcus Borg), the roster of fellows by no means represents the cream of New Testament scholarship in this country. Of the major *graduate* New Testament faculties, only Claremont is presently represented. Emory University had one participant for a time. Otherwise, the roster of fellows includes no present faculty at Yale, Harvard, Princeton, Duke, Union, Emory, or Chicago. The faculties at such schools are not necessarily hostile to the Seminar's work, but no members of those faculties are participants. The Seminar does not include established scholars from England or the Continent, although it does have some members from Canada and South Africa. Most of the participants are in relatively undistinguished academic positions. Some are not in the strict sense in academic positions at all.

These observations do not reflect on the seriousness or ability of the members. They are meant only to deflate the sometimes grandiose claims made by and for the Seminar as representing critical New Testament scholarship. It patently does no such thing. What becomes clear from scanning the academic training of the participants is that they overwhelmingly come from a cluster of graduate programs in New Testament that have in recent decades championed the sort of methodological and ideological stances reflected in the Seminar's work. Forty of the seventy-four fellows listed by *The Five Gospels* received their doctorates from five schools: fourteen from Claremont, nine from Vanderbilt, eight from Harvard, five from Chicago, and four from Union Theological Seminary.

The Jesus Seminar has been more provocative stylistically than substantively. In substance, the group has proceeded like many other task forces devoted to a particular subject: papers are prepared and read, discussion and debate follow, and the participants reach some sort of consensus before moving on to the next stage. Such processes are found widely in translation committees and in groups studying specific Gospels or the development of biblical traditions. The SBL has workshops and seminars devoted to such topics as "The Sources of the Pentateuch," for example, or "The Composition of Q" (a hypothetical source for the Gospels of Matthew and Luke).

Neither was taking on the subject of the historical Jesus particularly innovative. A good portion of New Testament critical scholarship since David Strauss's 1835 book, *The Life of Jesus Critically Examined,* had touched in one way or another on this subject. Indeed, one of the great moments in twentieth-century New Testament scholarship was Albert Schweitzer's *Quest of the Historical Jesus* (1906), which traced the efforts of scholars since the late eighteenth century to determine the historical character of Jesus' ministry. That first quest was followed by a much quieter "Second Quest" in the 1960s. The Jesus Seminar likes to think of itself as the vanguard of the "Third Quest."

The approach of the Seminar is not unique or obviously shocking, either. Like a great deal of Gospel criticism, it began with the assumption that the Gospels are not accurate histories but are narratives constructed out of traditional materials with literary art and theological motives. The Seminar therefore devotes attention to the separate strands of tradition within the Gospels, testing each strand individually according to criteria of historicity (more on these, later). It spent its first years—the ones here being reviewed—looking at the sayings of Jesus rather than at his deeds. All of these decisions, while arguable, are within the framework of scholarly inquiry.

The Seminar has drawn so much attention not because of its innovative science but because of its deliberately provocative style. The style of the Seminar's proceedings has been, from its inception, what most distinguishes it from other scholarship. At each meeting, participants voted with colored beads for the probability of a particular saying's authenticity. No more effective way to draw attention could be imagined. Scholars are *voting* on the contents of the gospel! As Funk himself pointed out (*Los Angeles Times,* 13 Dec. 1992), such voting takes place in other scholarly settings, such as translation committees. But as he also noted, these votes are carried out privately. Now, the voting is itself part of the show. Funk noted in another interview what fun it was: "Anyone who interprets literature or philosophy just isn't used to making a decision about anything. They find it exhilarating just to have to make up their minds about something" (*Christian Century,* 23 Nov. 1988).

The voting was not only public, it was *color-coded*, with each color having its own clever and colloquial interpretation:

red: That's Jesus!

pink: Sure sounds like Jesus.

gray: Well, maybe.

black: There's been some mistake.

Something more than cleverness is involved here. Those who have dismissed the procedure have missed its real significance. First, it is a process biased against the authenticity of the Gospel traditions. It is in the very nature of scholars to vie with one another to be more critical, to be "harder graders." The procedure forces sayings to *prove* their authenticity, rather than their authenticity being assumed and the burden of proof being placed on showing inauthenticity. Second, the voting process creates a competition among sayings that is similar to an election: who will win? Was it any surprise that the media, which covers American elections largely in terms of winning and losing, would focus precisely—as it was programmed to do—on this aspect of the Seminar's work? The voting mechanism was a deliberate attention-creating device.

The Seminar has also been distinctive for its "road show" appearances. In its twice-yearly meetings, it has traveled the country, beginning with its first meeting in 1985 at the obscure St. Meinrad School of Theology in southern Indiana, touching down on campuses such as the University of Redlands in 1986 and Luther Northwestern in 1987, and moving on to Atlanta (1988) and Rutgers University (1991). The visitation of local sites has also helped fuel media attention precisely by bringing something "newsworthy" to the local religion pages. And the Seminar showed itself unusually willing to involve the media. The press was invited to observe proceedings, and Seminar spokespersons were always ready to be interviewed. Moreover, since each seminar dealt with a discrete section of materials, and each separate vote was reported in the press and gained its own response, the entire process became a self-generating and self-renewing media event. From one perspective, the Jesus Seminar can be regarded as one of the most brilliant prepublication campaigns for a book ever devised. It would be hard to find (outside of Selznick's quest for Scarlett) a longer or more elaborate tease of public interest in service of selling a product (*The Five Gospels*).

Magister Ludi

The ringmaster-entrepreneur behind the Seminar has undoubtedly been Robert Funk. He has set its goals, been its most active spokesperson, and received the most media attention. The Seminar has, to a great extent, carried out the agenda set for it by Funk's keynote address at the first meeting in 1985, as reported in the Seminar's publication *Forum* 1/1 (1985) under the title, "The Issue of Jesus." Funk there begins with a complaint against the established church: "The religious establishment has not allowed the intelligence of high scholarship to pass through pastors and priests to a hungry laity" (p. 8). More specifically, he objects to the way television evangelists have "preyed on the ignorance of the uninformed." He sees the work of the Seminar, therefore, as spelling "liberty for . . . millions."

From the start, then, we see that the agenda of the Seminar is not disinterested scholarship, but a social mission against the way in which the church controls the Bible, and the way in which the church is dominated by a form of evangelical and eschatological theology—that is, a theology focused both on the literal truth of the Gospels and the literal return of Jesus—that Funk finds intolerable. It is important to note from the start that Funk does not conceive of the Seminar's work as making a contribution to scholarship but as carrying out a cultural mission.

Funk complains that New Testament scholars "have not fulfilled their obligation to report their work to a larger public . . . [they] have limited their pronouncements to the classroom or buried their considered judgments in scientific journals and technical jargon . . . they have hesitated to broadcast the *assured results of historical critical scholarship* out of fear of public controversy and political reprisal" (*Atlanta Journal,* 11 Nov. 1985; emphasis added). We see, then, that the Seminar's primary purpose is not to discover things, but to disseminate things already known. The proper image of Jesus is already assumed. It is the one that contradicts that of the televangelists. All that is required is to make this public. The technique of public voting is to draw attention to the proper construal (or interpretation) of Jesus, and is therefore a form of advertising. Funk's interpretation is revealingly disingenuous: "The voting tends to identify trends in research that otherwise might not show up for years if limited to the much slower process of waiting for findings to be published in journals and books" (*Washington Post,* 22 Oct. 1988).

Funk sees his goal as one of liberating Jesus from the Gospels, and the public from its thrall to dogma. "It isn't Jesus bashing . . . we want to liberate Jesus. The only Jesus most people want is the mythic one. They don't want the real Jesus. They want the one they can worship. The cultic Jesus" (*Los Angeles Times,* 24 Feb. 1994, View section). The "real Jesus" for Funk, therefore, is different from the one worshiped by Christians. Another quotation from Funk in the *San Jose Mercury News* (12 Feb. 1994) shows how he regards the process of Gospel composition: "Matthew, Mark, Luke and John 'marketed the Messiah' to make him conform to Christian doctrine that evolved after the death of Jesus . . . a man, ironically, who rebelled against the doctrine of his time." Funk explains the "pink" vote thusly: "Pink suggests that the original words have been altered or edited to suit the later social circumstances of the rapidly spreading Christian movement" (*Washington Post,* 9 Mar. 1991). He obviously does not regard such alteration to be the work of the Holy Spirit or even of a benign impulse. He declares, "If I were a leader of this fledgling community of Christians and wanted my views remembered, I'd attribute them to Jesus" (*U.S. News & World Report,* 1 July 1991).

It does not require too great a stretch to see Funk's dream of a purified "Five Gospels" as a distinct "marketing of the Messiah" in competition to that found in the canonical Gospels. In fact, he states concerning the publication of *The Five Gospels* that he hopes it will find its way into church pews and the hands of laypeople: "It should be helpful to anyone who is looking for a different approach to biblical material, *based on hard historical evidence*" (*U.S. News & World Report,* 1 July 1991). I added the italics to the last phrase simply to point out the inconsistency running through all these statements. On the one hand, Funk wants the Seminar's work to be seen as rigorously academic and "historical"; but on the other hand, as the statements below indicate, he is well aware that the image of Jesus being put forward by the Seminar is fictive.

In fact, Funk is quoted (*U.S. News & World Report,* 8 Nov. 1993) as stating that the Bible is a "cultural artifact" and that scholars have the "moral responsibility to determine what belongs to the fundamental cultural legacies of Christianity and Judaism." By what criteria should *scholars* perform this cultural rescue? According to Funk's opening statement to the Seminar in 1985, the criteria are provided by the worldview of enlightenment: "We are having increasing difficulty these days in accepting the biblical account of the creation and of the apocalyptic conclusion in anything like a literal sense" (*Forum* 1/1, 1985, p. 11). Ah. So we see that eschatology in general is something that Funk (and presumably his colleagues) has "increasing difficulty in accepting." Will we then be surprised to find that the Seminar's Jesus lacks any trace of eschatology?

Funk is nothing if not candid in addressing the "problem" that Jesus poses for those whose belief in creation or eschatology has disappeared: "To put the matter bluntly, we are having as much trouble with the middle—the Messiah—as we are with the terminal points. *What we need is a new fiction* that takes as its starting point the central event in the Judaeo-Christian drama and reconciles that middle with a new story that reaches beyond old beginnings and endings. In sum, we need a new narrative of Jesus, *a new Gospel,* if you will, that places Jesus differently in the grand scheme, the epic story" (*Forum* 1/1, 1985, p. 12; emphasis added).

These statements from the Seminar's founder at the group's inception make it clear that any pretense the Seminar has maintained with regard to scientific discovery was, at least in Funk's view, merely pretense: the results were already determined ahead of time. The goal was the construction of a new Gospel that portrayed a noneschatological and "nonmythical" Jesus. Funk's language is certainly straightforward: "Our fictions, though deliberately fictive, are nevertheless not subject to proof or falsification" (*Forum* 1/1, 1985, p. 11). So much for the elaborate process of testing for authenticity and voting! And he adds: "We need a fiction that we recognize to be fictive" (p. 12).

Funk's statements reveal a strange combination of grandiosity and hucksterism. Immediately preceding these grand remarks on the Seminar's cultural-salvage operation, Funk reveals a fear of irrelevance and a rage at academic powerlessness: "If we are to survive as scholars of the Humanities, as well as Theologians, we must quit the academic closet. And we must begin to sell a product that has some utilitarian value to someone . . . or which at least *appears* to have utilitarian value to someone" (*Forum* 1/1, 1985, p. 10; emphasis added). Is this statement really as cynical as it sounds? In any case, it is clear that any service rendered is not to the institutional church: "To learn that the Jesus of the Gospel of John is a figment of the evangelist's imagination or that Paul is not the author of the Pastoral Epistles goes down poorly with ecclesiastical officials, who are more concerned with membership and the collection plate than with the historical truth" (*San Francisco Chronicle*, 9 Mar. 1986). Funk's caricature of the church misses the real concern that greeted his Seminar's efforts, and masks the obvious need for power that runs through the Seminar's round of self-display. Both aspects are well stated by a dissenting voice from within the Seminar at one of its early meetings. It is attributed to John Williams (whom the article associates with Syracuse University): "We imitate those we take as our opponents—even though we think they are wrong, they have something we want. Usually this is the desire for power of some sort . . . faith does not demand the words of Jesus. It demands an understanding of ourselves and each other in light of Jesus *and* the early Christian witness" (*San Francisco Chronicle*, 9 Mar. 1986; emphasis in original).

Media Coverage

To appreciate the media's response to the Jesus Seminar, it is necessary to remember some things about the media in this country. Most obvious is that it is increasingly geared to coverage of the ephemeral. Two principles govern the professional ethics of the media: get it first and get it right. If a news organization cannot get earliest coverage of breaking news, then it seeks exclusive coverage of some aspect of the event. Few newspapers or local television stations have the resources to do in-depth reporting on any issue. Recent coverage of politics is symptomatic: long-range issues are hard to get at, but horse-race elections are easy to cover. Policy is boring, but the downfall of a politician is juicy. The borderline between news and entertainment is almost nonexistent; both have increasingly been centered in the personal and the scandalous.

In such a context, the coverage of religion is particularly problematic. Religion is, generally, the chronically non-news area of culture. Religion's stock-in-trade is continuity and world stabilization; its natural tendency is to celebrate the created order more than to subvert the social order. There is not much in the liturgical year to raise eyebrows or sell papers. Religion does not lend itself to front-page or top-of-broadcast coverage. If newspapers and television stations

cannot cover politics in depth—even with official political reporters and columnists—how can they cover religion with any degree of adequacy? Besides, it's
boring. Being religion editor of the daily paper is like being the Maytag repair-
man in the TV commercials. You mainly watch the store and reprint the bul-
letins. The only time religion can be called real news is when there is a scandal
or when a personality is involved. Best of all is a personal scandal: the tribulations of Jim Bakker and Jimmy Swaggart are followed obsessively. And when a
cult is involved, happiness reigns: now there is cultural significance, scandal,
and usually a charismatic personality. The David Koresh–Branch Davidian
apocalypse was terrific news . . . and it was religious! Roman Catholicism always gets good press for the election of a pope, which has gossip, votes, and
personalities.

Otherwise, the yearly cycle for the religion pages is all too drearily predictable. And Christianity, the dominant religion in the culture, is the worst. Judaism can be counted on for the High Holy Days with interesting pictures. A
local ashram can liven the pages once in a while. But Christianity is simply too
well known to be news. Any professor of religion in this country—especially
professors of New Testament—can bear witness to the twice-yearly calls from
religion editors: "It's Christmas: can you comment on the infancy accounts?"
Or, "It's Easter: anything new on the resurrection?" An air of quiet desperation
surrounds the entire interview: the editor needs copy; the academic—who fears
that an appropriately nuanced answer will be rendered as mush or distortingly
oversimplified—wants only to get back to correcting papers.

Into this dismal situation blew the Jesus Seminar. It wanted coverage! It
sought coverage! It understood deadlines! It invited media response! Best of
all, it provided colored beads, the closest thing (outside the Vatican) that religion ever provided to an actual election, *plus* provocative statements crafted
into usable sound bites! As a bonus, it dealt not with hard-to-cover issues like
sin and grace, but with a *personality*, the founding figure himself, Jesus! And
to bring it all home, it promised, vote by vote, statement by statement, the
shape of a scandalous attack on the foundations of Christianity. The conscious crafting of the Jesus Seminar into a media darling could not but be embraced by a segment of the media starved for the chance to do real news.

A so-called academic seminar, supposedly devoted to the soberest historical research, but actually desirous of exerting power over or within the Christian church, and consciously designed to be a media juggernaut, meets a group of religion reporters with more than a slight professional interest in the Seminar's work. Indeed, one of the reporters who first gave extensive coverage to the Seminar was John Dart of the *Los Angeles Times,* himself the author of a book sympathetic to the construction of an alternative Jesus (see *The Jesus of Heresy and History,* Harper & Row, 1988). All that was needed for the culture wars to begin was to fire the first salvos and await return fire from the churches.

Robert Funk himself was always the first and best source of lively quotations. Sometimes he was the soul of academic probity: the Seminar wanted "to inquire simply and rigorously after the *voice* of Jesus, after what he really said" (*Christianity Today,* 12 Dec. 1986; emphasis in original). The Seminar was not made up of unbelievers, he said; the participants "represent a wide spectrum of religious belief . . . the fellows include an ample number of both Catholics and Protestants" (*U.S. Catholic,* Sept. 1989). Funk could also be reassuring: ". . . quite a number of events in the Gospels probably have some historical core" (*Los Angeles Times,* 30 Mar. 1991). And he could assess the Seminar's purposes in terms of service to the church and academy: "We were obviously successful in making the public more aware of what biblical scholarship says, in contradistinction to the literal interpretation of television evangelists . . . I have a strong sense that my colleagues have accepted a new responsibility to give an accounting to the public" (*Los Angeles Times,* 30 Mar. 1991).

In a more defensive posture, he is aware that the fellows "are going to look bad when people say we don't believe in the Bible" (*Atlanta Journal,* 11 Nov. 1985). He refers to "my critics" and says that they "really object to having Jesus say anything about Christianity. They think we should stick to a creed that denies Jesus any voice at all" (*San Jose Mercury News,* 12 Feb. 1994). He declares that "I've had people call me a pawn of Satan, or say I'm Satan himself" (*Los Angeles Times,* 13 Dec. 1992).

Funk might have had a better sense of his critics' problems if he had assessed the cumulative impact of his and his colleagues' declarations, as they appeared in the daily papers. Funk states baldly, ". . . way less than 25% of the words attributed to Jesus were his" (*Los Angeles Times*, 5 Mar. 1989). He states that the goal of the Seminar is to "look for the real Jesus as close as we can find," but then adds, ". . . then we will look at why the church adapted Jesus to fit its needs. We are not looking for the Jesus who is easy for Americans in the 20th century" (*Atlanta Journal-Constitution*, 30 Sept. 1989). In the same interview, he states that "the role of Mark is greatly diminished in establishing who Jesus really was," and that "seminar participants believe Jesus did not describe an apocalyptic return." Concerning the resurrection, Funk declares offhandedly, "I am reasonably certain that the Fellows are going to say that the resurrection happened as a vision to followers such as Peter, James and Paul" (*Los Angeles Times*, 30 Mar. 1991).

Could Funk really have been surprised that such casual characterizations, obiter dicta as sound bites, would generate a sense of shock and outrage among readers who had a commitment to the tradition? What did he imagine they would think when he declared that Jesus' message is "buried in the Bible. We're trying to release Jesus, to free him up again so he can say what he has to say about the tradition" (*San Jose Mercury News*, 12 Feb. 1994)? How did he suppose such readers would react when told Funk's idea of how a movie about Jesus should portray him: his "only real friends are the religious, economic, and moral outcasts of society," and in the end "he is accidentally crucified along with other rabble-rousers" (*Washington Post*, 12 Nov. 1988)? How did Funk suppose this characterization would find acceptance among the pious: "This Jesus was a social gadfly, upsetting now this, now that, convention . . . he was clearly no conserver of traditional values; he was no goody-two-shoes" (*Atlanta Journal-Constitution*, 30 Sept. 1989); or this one: Jesus is "something of a party-animal" (*Los Angeles Times*, 13 Dec. 1992)? Did he imagine that such folk would also then take seriously his protestation that "We're trying to put the mystery back into the religion that bears Jesus' name" (*San Jose Mercury News*, 12 Feb. 1994)? Did he think that no offense would be taken by his having stated that ordinary Christians "don't want the real Jesus. They want one they can worship. The cultic Jesus" (*Los Angeles Times*, 24 Feb. 1994, View section)? Did he imagine that his own characterization of the "real Jesus" would be viewed as the deduction of serious scholarship and piety: "a sort of flower child with an idealistic view of life that is virtually impossible to achieve . . . more than half the members of the Seminar believe that Jesus probably was not celibate, that he did not advocate celibacy as a lifestyle, and that he had a 'special' relationship with at least one woman, but that it may not have been a sexual relationship" (*Atlanta Journal,* 30 Sept. 1989)?

As I page through the file of clippings from which I am working, I know that some readers might object to my procedure. Why such a focus on Funk? And why draw on statements from press reports, especially when they are obviously quoted out of context? It is appropriate to assert in response to such objections that I have no personal knowledge of Funk at all, nor any reason to consider him as anything but a worthy person. He is known to me only as he has made himself known through this media machine that I am analyzing. My analysis is of Funk as he appears in these discrete statements. I focus on him because he is the voice most often quoted, from beginning to end, and because he appears in these stories as the *magister ludi,* the coordinator of the game. If my reader objects that a selection of random comments taken out of narrative context does not lead to an understanding of the "real Funk," I shall be delighted. For I would then ask my reader if the application of the same procedure with the Gospels is any more likely to yield the "real Jesus."

Funk was by no means the only Jesus Seminar participant quoted in the papers. But his style of discourse continues in the comments of others. Karen King of Occidental College is quoted reassuringly, "Our motives are not to be destructive of faith, nor does anyone think we could be . . . but scholars do not want to sacrifice intellectual integrity for a naive approach to the texts" (*Atlanta Journal,* 11 Nov. 1985). All the more unfortunate that another quotation attributed to Professor King does not automatically suggest intellectual rigor; referring to the parable of Lazarus and Dives in Luke 16:19–31, her tone is dismissive and casual: "This parable is so banal . . . it's almost too convenient that Luke has just picked up something that suits him" (*San Francisco Chronicle,* 9 Mar. 1986). Since when is "nonbanality" a criterion of historicity?

Hal Taussig was a United Methodist Church pastor in Philadelphia when he was quoted as saying that the Seminar was providing "good, objective information about Jesus" for Christians who "feel threatened by Fundamentalism" (*Atlanta Journal,* 11 Nov. 1985). Then he was a professor at St.

Joseph's University in Pennsylvania when he gave one of the papers at the Seminar on the Lord's Prayer—according to the *Christian Century* (23 Nov. 1988), the paper on which the subsequent vote was based. The Seminar voted that the Lord's Prayer did not come from Jesus. Among the reasons offered was the one by Professor Steven Patterson of Eden Theological Seminary that it was unlikely Jesus wanted to compose a set prayer, since the Gospels show he often objected to religious rituals and formulas (*Atlanta Constitution*, 15 Oct. 1988). Not only does such a statement require dependence on the narrative portions of the Gospels that the Seminar had not yet considered, but in fact it would be difficult to support from the evidence of the Gospels themselves. But (now professor) Taussig had the most compelling quote on this issue, revealing the exact level of academic precision characterizing the debate: "I think he [Jesus] prayed, but I don't think he made a big deal out of it" (*Atlanta Constitution*, 15 Oct. 1988).

Although the noteworthy sound bites are almost endless, only a few more can be considered. Discussing the fact that all but three lines in John's Gospel were assigned "black" votes (meaning that it was all the work of the church), and those three were only assigned gray to show that the sayings attributed to Jesus were in agreement with his basic message, Professor Robert Fortna asserts confidently, "Most scholars, if they would work through the sayings as we had, would tend to agree that there is virtually nothing in [John] that goes back to Jesus" (*Washington Post*, 9 Mar. 1991). Once more, the colloquial and imprecise language puzzles the careful reader. Does Fortna mean that if scholars worked through the materials at all, or if the scholars worked through them *in the way the Seminar did?* Certainly, scholars as nontraditional as J. A. T. Robinson of *Honest to God* fame worked through the Johannine material (in *The Priority of John*) with much greater confidence in their historicity than Fortna. But if he means *in the way the Seminar did,* does he suggest that the game was rigged, that the rules of the Seminar made everything in John doomed from the start? Does he really mean that although the Seminar had only considered the sayings material, it can state categorically that "virtually nothing" in John goes back to Jesus? And did the Seminar in effect decide that if the *wording* of a saying qualified it to be assigned to the black, then there was no sense at all in which it "went back to Jesus"? All these implications seem embedded in Fortna's offhand remark, yet none of them are supported by the votes actually taken. In any case, such offhandedness itself is a reason why, as Fortna notes in the same interview, the results "will be startling to most people and deeply offensive to many, not just fundamentalists" (*Washington Post*, 9 Mar. 1991).

The most irritating feature of the Seminar may have been its indulgence in cute and casual discourse concerning matters of considerable historical moment and genuine religious concern. What are readers of newspapers to think when they read a quotation like this from Professor Dennis MacDonald of Iliff School of Theology: "Are we still too romantic about Jesus as a great figure? Jesus spoke all of these things to a community of believers who were there to hear his message and shape it" (*San Francisco Chronicle*, 9 Mar. 1986)? MacDonald's statement admittedly is cited out of context in the newspaper account. But standing isolated, it makes him appear to hold a position like that of Burton Mack (who will be considered in the next chapter) in regarding Jesus as a less than "great figure." If Jesus were actually the sort of person suggested by a Seminar participant called Leif Vaage, then a Lutheran pastor in Lima, Peru, now a New Testament professor at Emmanuel College at the University of Toronto, maybe that would be preferable: Vaage declares that Jesus was very likely "a party animal, somewhat shiftless, and disrespectful of the fifth commandment: Honor your father and mother" (*Atlanta Constitution*, 30 Sept. 1989). It is hard to avoid the impression that statements such as these are deliberately intended to shock and, in the fashion of naughty schoolchildren, draw attention.

In response to the perception that the Seminar was troubling people's faith, John Dominic Crossan, the Seminar's co-chair, delivered this opinion: "The person whose faith can be shaken by scholarship has a pretty shaky faith to begin with" (*Newsweek*, 31 Oct. 1988). But isn't this fairly cynical, when spoken by the leader of a Seminar that has declared explicit war on a certain version of Christian faith (that of fundamentalists, televangelists) in the name of "scholarship," and has, in its self-presentation, the goal of purifying faith precisely by scholarship?

The media-circus dimension of the Jesus Seminar is nowhere shown more clearly than in the participation of Paul Verhoeven, whose Ph.D. is from the

University of Leiden but whose professional affiliation is with Brooksfilms as a movie director, and whose credits include *Robocop, Basic Instinct,* and *Showgirls.* Verhoeven, according to the *Washington Post* (12 Nov. 1988), plans to produce a movie about Jesus based on the findings of the Jesus Seminar, whose members would thereby become "consultants." The presence of Hollywood has had its usual effect, described in delicious detail by Russell Shorto in a profile called "Cross Fire" that appeared in *GQ* (June 1994). Shorto depicts the scholars pitching various cinematic possibilities to an "impassive" Verhoeven, who listens to one after another before breaking "into a little smile. 'Yeah,' he says, 'I'll do it that way, probably.'" The circle has turned full. The Seminar that courted the attention of the media has succeeded beyond its dreams. The talk now is not of Matthew and Mark, but of *The Last Temptation of Christ,* and of Scorsese and Zeffirelli. This is real importance and power. Forget shaping scholarship. Forget renewing the church. We're gonna make a movie! The further development of Verhoeven's plans, which turned out to envisage a very eschatological Jesus, drawn in large measure from the Gospel of John, as well as the dismay these aroused in some Seminar participants, is detailed in an article by Charlotte Allen, "Away with the Manger" (*Lingua Franca: The Review of Academic Life,* Feb. 1995, pp. 22–30). As Allen sardonically remarks, "despite eight years of faithful attendance at the Jesus Seminar, he hadn't been paying much attention" (p. 27).

All these noises were faithfully reported by the press. And following its normal practice, the press also gave abundant space to the detractors and opponents of the Jesus Seminar. Church representatives in the various locales where the Seminar pitched its tent were regularly solicited for sound bites to match those emitted by the Seminar spokespersons. Some ministers expressed cautious or enthusiastic support for the Seminar. The Reverend Tom Conley of the Northside Drive Baptist Church in Atlanta said he "would agree wholeheartedly" with the Seminar (*Atlanta Journal-Constitution,* 16 Oct. 1988). The Reverend Edward Beutner, campus minister at Santa Clara, declared that "they are not maverick scholars . . . they take a very careful approach to how the sayings of Jesus were transmitted and to the evolution of biblical texts" (*U.S. Catholic,* Sept. 1985). Arland Jacobsen, director of the Charis Ecumenical Center at Concordia College, Moorhead, Minnesota, insisted that the

Seminar was expressing the implicit views of most ministers: ". . . when there is surprise by churchgoers at Jesus Seminar findings, it is often because pastors don't share those assumptions with their congregations" (*Los Angeles Times*, 30 Mar. 1993). Jacobsen's comment is a provocative one, and I will return in chapter 3 to the issue it raises.

More often, however, the press reported negative comments from church representatives. Many of these were as pungent as the sound bites from the Seminar. A certain Rev. R. L. Hymers is quoted in the *Los Angeles Times Magazine* (13 Dec. 1992) to the effect that the Seminar members are "a bunch of damn fools." Pat Robertson of the television "700 Club" called the Seminar "outrageous" and characterized the participants as trying to "accommodate the Bible to their own unbelief" (*Los Angeles Times*, 30 Mar. 1991). Marvin Reynolds of Los Osos, California, stated that the Seminar was "robbing the church of its blessed hope" and attributed its destructive power to the fact that "our society tends to place scholars on a very high level" (*Los Angeles Times*, 5 Mar. 1989). Paige Patterson, of the Criswell Center for Biblical Studies in Dallas, described the fellows as "condescending" toward the Bible and called their methods "about as scientific as a flat earth theory" (*Atlanta Journal-Constitution*, 23 May 1987). Bishop Earl Paulk, of the Chapel Hill Harvester Church in Decatur, Georgia, responded to the reports from the Seminar this way: "For the common person in the pew, it's tampering with their faith. It's important to me to touch people with a spiritual dimension. And to me, this does not engender hope or faith" (*Atlanta Journal-Constitution*, 16 Oct. 1988). The Reverend H. B. Thompson, the Georgia general overseer of the Church of God, called the Seminar's work "totally unchristian . . . I believe the Bible is the infallible word of God. All evangelical Christians I know do. That's certainly the stance of the Church of God" (*Atlanta Journal-Constitution*, 30 Sept. 1989). The Reverend Terry Payton of Dallas declared, "It's scary . . . my belief is that you either accept the whole Bible or you don't" (*Los Angeles Times*, 30 Mar. 1991). And Rev. James Eggert, the pastor of the First Baptist Church of Downey, California, responded: "Many young people are not well-versed enough to know the differences between liberal and conservative scholars. They wonder what's going on" (*Los Angeles Times*, 30 Mar. 1991).

The press also solicited the views of other New Testament scholars concerning the work of the Seminar. Some expressed muted approval. Karen Jo Torjeson, director of Women's Studies in Religion at Claremont, said, "I like to see the discussion carried out to the broader community" (*Los Angeles Times*, 30 Mar. 1991), and Carolyn Osiek, of the Catholic Theological Union in Chicago, declared, "These are first-class, top-flight scholars who reach their conclusions by consensus" (*U.S. Catholic*, Sept. 1989). Other New Testament scholars were far more reserved. Some objections came, as might be expected, from those teaching in conservative seminaries. It is not surprising to find Professor Don Carson of Trinity Evangelical Seminary characterize the work of the Seminar in terms of "left-wing ideology" that rejects anything supernatural and engages in circular arguments (*U.S. News & World Report*, 1 July 1991). One would expect Professor Don Hagner of Fuller Theological Seminary to state, "They can scheme away till they are blue in the face, but it's not going to change the church" (*U.S. News & World Report*, 8 Nov. 1993).

But scholars of impeccable critical credentials also were willing to go on the record concerning the Seminar. Joseph Fitzmyer of the Catholic University of America recognized that some notable scholars were involved with the project but that he would "apply the same standard of healthy skepticism to their work as to that of any scholar—that is, I find their conclusions interesting but certainly not beyond criticism or questioning" (*U.S. Catholic*, Sept. 1989). Walter Brueggeman of Columbia Theological Seminary was equally cautious: "I guess it's legitimate, but . . . highly subjective," and, "The Seminar is still trying to get behind the text, and I think that what we need to do is deal with the text" (*Atlanta Journal-Constitution*, 5 Mar. 1989). Jack Dean Kingsbury of Union Theological Seminary in Richmond, Virginia, was quoted as saying, "If the public thinks that scholars are being destructive rather than constructive, then the Seminar will have done the church a disservice" (*Washington Post*, 22 Oct. 1988). The most vehement response to the Seminar by a critical scholar with an international reputation was that of Howard Clark Kee, who in a letter to the *Los Angeles Times* declared the Seminar "an academic disgrace" (30 Mar. 1991; see also *U.S. News & World Report*, 1 July 1991). The press also faithfully covered a counterconference called "Jesus Christ: God and Man," involving some thirty historians and theologians, that was held at

Dallas Baptist University and sponsored in part by the journal *Truth*. At the conference, Paul Johnson, R. T. France, Francois Dreyfuss, and James Dunn in various ways responded negatively to the Seminar's work (*Christianity Today*, 16 Jan. 1987).

In all this coverage, the press proceeded fairly enough. It published the pronouncements and gathered the positive and negative responses. The press could, however, have been faulted for not more explicitly challenging the obviously media-savvy procedures of the Seminar, as noted by Gustav Niebuhr in an article entitled, "The Jesus Seminar Courts Notoriety" (*Christian Century*, 23 Nov. 1988), in which he observes how the vote "deciding" the authenticity of the Lord's Prayer was "just in time for the weekend papers and touched off an immediate response, particularly in the South."

More tellingly, the press coverage played into the Seminar's own agenda. Bruce Buursma, for example, reports the fact that John Lown of Point Loma Nazarene College in San Diego "was forced by school officials to resign his faculty position last month," and continues, "Despite the mounting opposition, the scholars are vowing to proceed with their research" (*Chicago Tribune*, 15 Mar. 1986). The problem with this coverage is that it is dependent on the Jesus Seminar's own publicity (no statement is taken from the seminary) and accepts its own account of the situation. Likewise, Gustav Niebuhr offers this interpretive comment: ". . . the seminar's work already has aroused the ire of some religious conservatives" (*Atlanta Constitution*, 23 May 1987). This characterization might lead the reader to think that only "religious conservatives" objected to the Seminar's procedures, and helps solidify precisely the polarization programmed by the Seminar. Moreover, the press did not follow up to see whether any of the Seminar participants, far from being penalized by their participation in the Seminar, actually made rather impressive progress in their academic careers during this period.

It is above all in its use of headlines, however, that the press helped create precisely the sort of commotion the Seminar wanted. The *Washington Post* (31 Oct. 1987) reported a "furor" that was generated in St. Paul, Minnesota, when the Minneapolis–St. Paul papers "reported under a banner headline that the group of biblical scholars had decided by secret ballot that 'Jesus did not publicly proclaim himself as the Messiah,'" despite the fact that an official "vote" was still a meeting away. The headlines often present a picture starker and more negative even than the stories they introduce, thus performing a sort of preemptive interpretation for the less than critical reader. A sample: "Scholars Say Jesus Was Often Misquoted" (*San Francisco Chronicle*, 9 Mar. 1986); "Jesus Didn't Claim to Be Messiah, Scholars Say" (*San Francisco Chronicle*, 18 Oct. 1987); "Lord's Prayer Not Jesus's, Scholars Say," (*Atlanta Journal-Constitution*, 15 Oct. 1988); "Jesus Never Predicted His Return, Scholars Say," (*Atlanta Constitution*, 5 Mar. 1989); "Jesus Didn't Promise to Return, Bible Scholars Group Says" (*Los Angeles Times*, 5 Mar. 1989). What is remarkable about these headlines (and they could easily be multiplied) is that they all combine two features: first, they *negate* some part of the Jesus tradition, and second, the negation is attributed to *scholars*. The press helped stimulate precisely the sort of controversy that the Jesus Seminar sought, and became the arena for a confused culture war between church and academy.

The Five Gospels

The regular media coverage of the Jesus Seminar's meetings and reactions to them was only part of the commotion. Members of the Seminar such as Marcus Borg and John Dominic Crossan published their own versions of the historical Jesus, and a variety of other writers (Barbara Thiering, A. N. Wilson, Stephen Mitchell, Bishop Spong, Burton Mack) also helped stir the pot with provocative revisions of Jesus and Christian origins. These books will be considered in the next chapter. All these publications have come out since 1990. All were reviewed by the press. Major attention was drawn to the "historical Jesus phenomenon" by an article by Peter Steinfels, "Peering Past Faith to Glimpse the Jesus of History," that appeared in the *New York Times* (23 Dec. 1991).

In addition, participants in the Seminar and authors of Jesus books placed articles in a variety of journals. The articles, books, and reviews all helped to create the sense of a powerful movement that required still more coverage by the major popular news magazines. The measure of the level of interest is not so much the running of articles by *Time*, *Newsweek*, and *U.S. News & World Report* as the running of major articles by the *Atlantic Monthly*, the *Humanist*, *GQ*, and *Lingua Franca*.

Certainly the publication of *The Five Gospels: The Search for the Authentic Words of Jesus* (Macmillan, 1993), which presented itself as a new translation and commentary by Robert W. Funk, Roy W. Hoover, and the Jesus Seminar, represented a major event, the climax of the more-than-five-year tease initiated by the Jesus Seminar in 1985. Although the Seminar was pledged to turn next to the deeds of Jesus, the publication at last provided other scholars and interested readers a chance to assess the actual work that had so tantalizingly been publicized through the media.

Four aspects of the book make it distinctive. The first is its new translation of the four canonical Gospels and the *Gospel of Thomas*. The translation is deliberately iconoclastic. Jesus does not tell the leper, "I will it, be made clean," but "Okay—you're clean!" (Mark 1:40). The beatitude is not, "Blessed are you poor," but "Congratulations, you poor!" (Luke 6:20). The "salt of the earth" does not have "savor" but "zing" (Matt. 5:13). Jesus is not "Son of man," but "Son of Adam"; the Sabbath is not "made for man" but "made for Adam and Eve" (Mark 2:27–28). The translation presents itself as "more historical" and in closer touch with ancient social realities than more "ecclesiastical" translations. In some cases, this may be so. In other cases, the colloquial and slangy seem to be chosen for their own sake—and reflect the deliberate insouciance and irreverence of the Seminar's press conferences. The result is not always greater accuracy. "Adam and Eve," for example, may be a politically correct rendering of "man," but it obliterates the specific symbolic background of this Gospel expression.

A second feature of *The Five Gospels* is the infamous color-coding of Jesus' sayings, ostensibly the reason for the publication, since the book is flagged, "What Did Jesus Really Say?" As expected and advertised, very few sayings are marked in red (only about fifteen), with about seventy-five more receiving a pink rating ("Jesus said something like this"). The index makes clear that these designations resulted from the percentage of votes for one color or another. A saying that appears *only* in the *Gospel of Thomas*, for example ("Become passersby"), ended up in the gray category, but had exactly as many fellows voting that it was red/pink as it did voting that it was gray/black. In other words, what is represented as a "scholarly consensus" is in fact a plus–50 percent result in a ballot involving about thirty electors. If sixteen voted that the saying was authentic, and fourteen that it was not, then it was assigned "pink." The fifteen "red" sayings, in contrast, all have 75 percent or better.

A third aspect of this book is its inclusion of the *Gospel of Thomas* together with the four canonical Gospels of the New Testament. The *Gospel of Thomas* is one of the compositions discovered at Nag Hammadi in 1947. Written in Coptic, it consists of a series of discrete sayings of Jesus with no narrative framework. Although scholars debate whether the *Gospel of Thomas* should be regarded as "Gnostic," there is a fairly wide agreement that in its literary form it postdates the canonical Gospels and should probably be dated at the very earliest to the mid-second century. The main point of debate for most scholars is whether the *Gospel of Thomas*'s sayings are dependent on the canonical Gospel tradition or represent, in some cases, a tradition as early or earlier than that found in the canonical Gospels. The inclusion of this gospel side by side with Matthew, Mark, Luke, and John in this book is all the more interesting since the *Gospel of Thomas* does not include a significantly higher number of red sayings (five), all of which are found in the canonical Gospels as well. Its inclusion seems to make primarily a political or "culture wars" point: the Gospels are to be considered of value only insofar as they are sources for the Historical Jesus, and the Christian canon should be reconstructed on that basis.

The fourth aspect of *The Five Gospels* is its packaging. This consists of a long introduction and a series of short essays that take up various aspects of the Seminar's procedures and policies. In the introduction, the reader is treated to the same sort of messianism and its accompanying flashes of paranoia that characterize so many of the Seminar statements. The book is dedicated to Galileo (presumably as an example of revolutionary teaching that is oppressed), Thomas Jefferson (who, as we will see in the next chapter, also produced an expurgated version of the teachings of Jesus), and David Strauss (*The Life of Jesus Critically Examined*, 1835). The implication is plainly that this book shares both the radical and the controversial character of such antecedents. Mention is made of the Seminar's critics, including the "skeptical left wing" and the "fundamentalist right" (p. 5). Scholars who criticized the

Seminar's practice of voting with beads are dismissed as "elitist academic critics who deplored the public face of the Seminar" (p. 34). "Conservative Christian groups" are the cause of the loss of an academic position for "at least one Fellow of the Jesus Seminar." Southern Baptists and Lutherans have been "witch-hunting for scholars who did not pass their litmus tests. Public attack on members of the seminar is commonplace, coming especially from those who lack academic credentials" (p. 35).

But the same animus toward *any* form of traditional Christianity already detectable in Funk's statements reappears here as well. The Nicene Creed "appears to smother the historical Jesus." The creed came about as a result of the influence of Paul, "who did not know the historical Jesus" and for whom "Jesus the man played no essential role." Not only do these assertions lack demonstration, but the introduction then identifies the creed of Christianity as a form of "theological tyranny" (pp. 7–8). It is extraordinarily difficult to avoid the impression that the Seminar's declared enemies are not simply fundamentalists or the "dictatorial tactics of the Southern Baptist Convention" (p. 8), but all those who subscribe to any traditional understanding of Jesus as defined by the historic creeds of Christianity, that is, in some sense as risen Lord and Son of God. The title of the introduction, "The Search for the Real Jesus: Darwin, Scopes, and All That," makes it clear: unless one is willing to grant that the Christian creed is "theological tyranny" and acknowledge the "liberation of the historical Jesus" carried out by the Seminar as normative for the "cultural reality" called Christianity, then one is lumped with those who resisted evolution in the name of an anti-intellectual biblical literalism.

The introduction also contains a fascinating account of the history of research into the historical Jesus and the Seminar's perception of its own role in that history (pp. 2–5), in the form of "seven pillars of scholarly wisdom" assumed by the Seminar. The first four of these pillars, or stages, are recounted already in Albert Schweitzer's classic *Quest of the Historical Jesus* (1906): the decision to treat Jesus as a historical figure rather than through the lens of faith; the decision to privilege the synoptic Gospels rather than John; the decision to regard Mark as the earliest of the Synoptics on which the others depend; and the recognition of Q as an independent source used by both

Matthew and Luke. What is odder is that this path is termed "the tragic and heroic story of those who endeavored to break the church's stranglehold over learning." A more neutral assessment would recognize that a great deal of such scholarship took place within the boundaries of the faith. By no means has critical biblical scholarship been entirely resisted by the church. Indeed, we will have occasion to wonder whether critical scholarship has not, by the major traditions of Christianity, been all too uncritically accepted.

In any case, the introduction resumes the narrative with the remaining three pillars. These are, however, the special premises of the Jesus Seminar rather than widely held positions. The first is that Jesus was not an eschatological figure and that his understanding of the kingdom was noneschatological. Far from representing a consensus of scholarship, this is one of the "assumptions" of the Jesus Seminar fellows that puts them perhaps most at odds with other researchers into the historical Jesus. The next assumption is that there is a sharp contrast between written and oral cultures, and that Jesus must be considered exclusively in terms of an oral culture. Again, this represents a highly simplistic division of ancient culture that the majority of students of the Mediterranean world and of first-century Palestine would reject. The seventh pillar is that the burden of proof now falls on the side of authenticity; each statement must justify its being considered to have its origin with Jesus. This makes explicit what the Seminar's procedures implicitly guaranteed.

The introduction adds a final pillar: "Beware of finding a Jesus entirely congenial to you" (p. 5). What this seems to mean in effect is that a Jesus conformable to the perceptions of Christian faith must be disallowed in favor of a Jesus who is a cultural critic.

The introduction also lists some of the specific criteria used by the Seminar in reaching its decisions on historicity. Some of these are in fact the common criteria of those working with Gospel traditions. The criterion of multiple attestation, for example, is inarguable: the more independent sources that contain an element of tradition, the stronger is the probability that it is early, perhaps even from Jesus. Likewise, the criteria of dissimilarity and embarrassment are widely employed by other scholars: an element of tradition that is distinct either from the Judaism that preceded Jesus or the church that followed him is *logically* more likely to be from him than not, just as an element concerning Jesus that would cause embarrassment to the church would not likely have been invented by it.

Other criteria, however, are highly debatable, and raise questions concerning the Seminar's self-proclaimed objectivity. Is it really so, as it declares, that only short aphorisms can be remembered accurately—especially in an "oral culture"? Can it be assumed that Jesus "characteristically" spoke in short aphorisms, that he never initiated dialogue but only responded to others, that he was consistently paradoxical and countercultural in his outlook? It should be obvious that these are not "criteria" at all, but assumptions that are attached to a predetermined vision of the Jesus who is supposedly sought.

What sort of scholarship, then, do we find in *The Five Gospels?* It is not of an impressive quality. The most notable lack in the publication is any discernible *demonstration* or even *argument*. Much is asserted here without either evidence or even substantial logic. A reader not already converted to the Seminar's own perceptions finds no reason to accept its conclusions apart from its own insistence that it is fighting against the forces of darkness and suppression of truth. Something so fundamental as the eschatological character of Jesus' ministry or speech—that Jesus worked in view of a future triumph of God's will—is simply dismissed without significant argument. The introduction insists, for example, that although John the Baptist had an eschatological mission, and although the earliest Christian traditions understood Jesus eschatologically, Jesus the disciple of John (the Baptist) and teacher of the Church had a completely noneschatological and indeed countereschatological understanding of God's kingdom. A less sophisticated logic might naturally conclude just the opposite: if Jesus' mentor was eschatological and Jesus' followers were eschatological, it would seem logical to suppose that Jesus was eschatological!

The level of scholarship employed can be illustrated as well by the odd inclusion of the parable of the good Samaritan (Luke 10:30–35) among the "red" (authentic) sayings of Jesus. It is ranked ninth among the red sayings, with a positive approval of .81. But how can this be? It is found only in the Gospel of Luke, therefore failing to meet the (we thought essential) criterion of multiple attestation. Furthermore, it is fairly lengthy, certainly not a "short aphorism"—the only sort capable of being remembered accurately! More than that, it fits beautifully within the theological interests of Luke's Gospel, thus appearing as "banal" if judged by the same standards as Lazarus and Dives! Why then is it included? The only answer possible is that it fits the Seminar's preconceived notion of who Jesus must have been. The Seminar has not consistently followed the very criteria it established.

Far more questionable as legitimate historical inquiry is the sort of artificial compartmentalization of evidence essential to the Seminar's work. It is remarkable that the Seminar was prepared to make statements on who the "real Jesus" was simply on the basis of a handful of his sayings that it judged to be authentic. The rest of the New Testament evidence concerning Jesus and Christian origins is casually dismissed. Paul is caricatured as "having no interest in Jesus." The narratives of Acts and the Gospels are tossed out as mythical fabrications based on faith. More than that, any sayings that are "developed" must also be dismissed from the reconstruction. What is left is a small pile of pieces. But on this basis, Jesus is declared to have "really" been one way rather than another. And this is announced *before* the Seminar takes up its (equally portentous) work of figuring out which deeds attributed to Jesus "really" came from him. This is not responsible, or even critical, scholarship. It is a self-indulgent charade. As Professor Richard Hays of Duke University concluded in a lengthy review of this book ("The Corrected Jesus," *First Things*, May 1994, pp. 43–48), ". . . the case argued by this book would not stand up in any court. The critical study of the historical Jesus is an important task . . . but the *Five Gospels* does not advance that task significantly, nor does it represent a fair picture of the current state of research on this problem. Some of its purported revelations are old news, and many of its novel claims are at best dubious."

The publication of *The Five Gospels* explicitly reveals the saddest paradox about the Jesus Seminar. It has taken fundamentalism as its great enemy. But the Seminar ultimately shares the same literalism and historical positivism that characterize fundamentalism. Fundamentalists wrongly stake all Christian faith on the literal historical accuracy of the Bible. They insist that they read literally, but in fact they read everything within a set of "fundamen-tal convictions" concerning who Jesus must be. The Seminar's obsessive con-cern with historicity and its extreme literalism merely represents the opposite side of fundamentalism. Now, other "fundamental convictions" concerning who Jesus *must* be are taken to be "historically accurate" and therefore show-ing "the real Jesus." The portrait is different, but the technique in painting is the same. The paradox suggests that the connection between "history" and "faith" requires much closer analysis.

CHAPTER 2

History Challenging Faith

For all its notoriety, the Jesus Seminar has by no means held the stage alone. The flood of publications devoted to "the historical Jesus" since 1990 (to draw an artificial but necessary line) suggests that there has been a virtually endless appetite for books about Jesus, particularly in versions of his life that offer something secret or salacious, finally made available to a public that—we are to suppose—has been kept in ignorance by the powerful machinery of priestcraft.

Such books have followed a predictable pattern in their self-presentation, argument, claims, and promotion. The authors have, in addition to writing the books, produced pre- and postpublication articles on the same themes, have appeared on interview shows, and have had magazine articles devoted to profiles of them and their work. In the following pages, I will consider a selection, moving from publications that are less than responsible to ones that are far more substantial. The characterizations are sometimes overly brief, perhaps occasionally overly sharp. My purpose is not so much the dismissal of a single book as the defining of a larger pattern.

The Pattern

Barbara Thiering's *Jesus and the Riddle of the Dead Sea Scrolls: Unlocking the Secrets of His Life Story* (HarperSanFrancisco, 1992) exemplifies the pattern admirably. An obscure Australian academic whose credentials for addressing the question of the historical Jesus consist of four technical articles on the Dead Sea Scrolls and two books tracing the connections between Qumran and the Gospels, Thiering had her "research" made the subject of a television documentary on Palm Sunday, 1990, by the Australian Broadcasting Corporation. The commotion caused by that broadcast apparently led to the production of this book, which presents her full case.

What is her case? She argues that her reading of the Dead Sea Scrolls has given her the key to unlocking early Christian history: John the Baptist and Jesus are key figures in the history of the Qumran sect, and the method of interpretation developed in that sect, in turn, provides the clue to interpreting the Gospels. Thiering is not the first to propose connections between Qumran and the New Testament. But after an initial period of feverish speculation following the discovery of those documents in 1947, most studies have come to rather modest conclusions, considering the Qumran community and the nascent Christian movement to be analogous sectarian movements within Judaism, rather than directly connected. Thiering marks a return to untrammeled speculation. She argues that the history of Qumran and of early Christianity are the same. John the Baptist *is* the "Teacher of Righteousness" and Jesus *is* the "wicked priest" who opposed that teacher and was himself vilified in the scrolls.

This is bold indeed. Why has no one seen this before Thiering? Because their eyes were clouded by Christian belief in the uniqueness of the Gospel story. They were incapable of reading the texts appropriately. The Gospels are actually to be read, she claims, as forms of the *pesher* interpretation found in the Qumran sect's interpretation of Scripture: the events of the sect's history are read into and out of the texts of Torah. In similar fashion, the Gospels are giant cryptograms that can be unlocked only by reading them as *pesher:* the history of the sect is to be found in them, hidden beneath arcane symbolism. Once this step is taken, Thiering has the key to reading the Gospels as *real history* to which Christian faith has no access.

Since she now can move the pieces of the text around at will, Thiering has no problem recovering an elaborate "history." John and Jesus are both part of a grandiose political movement within Judaism. Jesus is born of Essene parents, John and Jesus split over the understanding of purity regulations, Jesus is crucified at Qumran and is buried in a cave there. But Jesus does not die. Thiering says that the gall in the wine offered him at the crucifixion was a slow-acting poison that made him appear to have died. In the tomb, Simon Magus, who was also crucified yet survived (this gets very complicated), crawls to Jesus through a tunnel between caves bringing aloe, a purgative that enables Jesus to expel the poison and thus recover—comfortably, since he was also administered myrrh to soothe his mucous membranes. Jesus then spends the next few years directing the church.

Thiering's "history" is the purest poppycock, the product of fevered imagination rather than careful analysis. The way she works with the data defies every canon of sober historical research, and operates outside all the rules of textual analysis. Her book is a classic example of a legitimate point, namely that the Qumran sectarians used events in their history as the key to interpreting some texts of Scripture, being developed into a grand explanatory scheme that the evidence simply cannot support. Yet her book was published in Australia and Great Britain, and then the United States. It did not appear in a shabby paperback version but in a handsome hardback complete with photographs and footnotes. It was not put out by a fly-by-night operation but originally in Australia and the United Kingdom by Doubleday and subsequently in the United States by Harper San Francisco, a publisher known for its production of mainstream reference works as well as cutting-edge New Testament scholarship (and, as it happens, the publisher of the present work as well—illustrating at least a solid commitment to freedom of speech!).

How can we account for the production of books like this? I think the answer is found in the way the book is presented. First, there is the emphasis placed on the scholarly credentials of the author, which are (explicitly or implicitly) contrasted to the traditional teaching of the church. Second, there is the offer of some novel angle on Jesus previously unknown and perhaps (more titillating still) "suppressed" by the church. Third, the truth about Jesus is offered through a "historical" reading of the Gospels—usually abetted by some perspective given by outside sources—that denies their surface meaning. Fourth, there is the suggestion that this new insight is provocative. Fifth, there is the implication that this new finding should cause Christianity to reexamine and perhaps revise its traditional teaching (see Thiering, pp. ix–xi, 1–4). The self-presentation of the book assumes and asserts a conflict between scholarship and the church, between history and faith.

Challenge and response are enabled by the communications media. The response is already programmed by prepublication blurbs that announce how "provocative" and "novel" this book will be. Postpublication marketing includes the solicitation of "responses" from local scholars and clergy through local media outlets. If these responses, as expected, are also "provocative" or "outraged," then there is *news*, and the media can ratchet up the volume another several notches in its coverage of the newly created "debate." The higher the pitch of controversy, the better business is for publishers, press, and the nightly news broadcast.

Amateur Night

Thiering at least claims to be a scholar. But Jesus books turned out by acknowledged amateurs are also handsomely produced. Two recent examples have been written by John Shelby Spong and A. N. Wilson. Neither author is a scholar, but each claims to be making available the work of critical scholarship. Neither author believes much of what the Gospels say about Jesus. They conceive of their chore in therapeutic terms. They seek to help those still enthralled by faith to find their way to the condition of enlightenment enjoyed by the authors.

Each writer also follows the predictable path of rationalist reduction. Historical difficulties in the texts as we have them are construed as hopeless obstacles, which must lead inevitably to skepticism. The void of skepticism is then filled with inventive speculation. The speculation is not a reasonable alternative reading based on the available evidence, but a complete reshuffling of the pieces, yielding a picture more satisfying to the aesthetic or religious sensibilities of the authors.

BISHOP JOHN SPONG

John Spong, an Episcopal bishop, has been for some years waging a rather public war against "fundamentalists," by whom he appears to mean anyone who takes the literal meaning of the New Testament texts seriously. He clearly conceives of himself as heir to the tradition of maverick Anglican and Episcopal bishops like J. A. T. Robinson and James Pike, who also had reputations for being radical and "provocative." His first foray into the Historical Jesus market was through *Born of a Woman: A Bishop Rethinks the Birth of Jesus* (HarperSanFrancisco, 1992). Both he and the publisher undoubtedly grasped and intended the provocative character of the book's subtitle, "A Bishop Rethinks the Birth of Jesus." The reader is primed to expect precisely the reductionistic rereading of the Gospels that Spong provides.

In Spong's "rethinking," the unexceptional observation that the infancy accounts of the Gospels are late in composition and yield little significant historical information—a position shared by such mainline scholars as R. E. Brown in his *Birth of the Messiah* (Doubleday, 1979)—quickly becomes the claim that "what really happened" has been "covered up" by the evangelists. If the virgin birth seems historically unlikely, one would think that a normal birth would be the logical alternative. In such a reading, Christians would have exercised the widespread Hellenistic practice of giving their hero (perceived in hindsight as extraordinary and indeed divine) an exceptional birth. But Spong's rage against "literalists," whose belief in the virgin birth and whose honor of Mary have apparently been responsible for every oppression against women in Western history, demands a conspiracy of more sinister character. Thus Spong's therapeutic rereading: Mary was "really" a teenaged girl who was raped and became pregnant with an illegitimate child. She was then taken under the protection of Joseph.

Spong is not so much interested, however, in what "really happened" as he is in freeing Christianity from its dogmatic entanglements, which he more or less identifies with fundamentalism. Spong is hostile to the birth narratives in the first case, he says, because they represent a displacement in Christianity, which made Christmas rather than Easter the focal event. But what is Easter for Spong? It appears to have been "not so much . . . a supernatural external miracle but . . . the dawning internal realization that this life of Jesus reflected a new image of God, an image that defied the conventional wisdom, an image that called into question the exalted king as the primary analogy by which God could be understood." The resurrection, it seems, is really a mental adjustment by the first disciples, a shift of their perception in the direction of the politically correct. But then Spong goes on to argue that Christians also got "Easter" wrong, since they concluded from the resurrection that Jesus was divine. Thus, if I have his argument right, the infancy accounts represent a further extension of the fundamental error that birthed Christianity.

Having a bishop with opinions like these is a bit like hiring a plumber who wants to "rethink pipes." Spong imagines that he has escaped his own fundamentalist past, but he has not. He remains defined by the literalism he so doggedly battles. His vaunted "liberalism" is in reality a tired rationalism. Readers who struggle on to the end through his repetitions, non sequiturs, and narcissistic self-referentiality are not really surprised to find Spong arguing that Jesus might have been married to Mary Magdalen, and that it was his own wedding at Cana for which he catered the wine. Bishop Spong seems to think that having Jesus born illegitimately and married to a prostitute will be received as good news by unliberated women everywhere.

Bishop Spong more recently has turned his attention to the other end of the Gospel story in *Resurrection: Myth or Reality?* (HarperSanFrancisco, 1994). The title is typically "provocative"; given his previous books, we can guess which is the right answer to the question posed by the subtitle. Once more, the reader is treated to the bishop's recital of his years of study with various scholars, to his attempts to fill the shoes of J. A. T. Robinson as the radical bishop of his generation, and to his asseverations of fidelity to the spiritual truth of resurrection even as he denies its literal reality.

Spong's textual key now is *midrash* (compare Barbara Thiering's *pesher*, above). When taken as literal history, that is, as telling about real events, the Gospels are misread. They are only properly understood as midrash, that is, as symbolic reworkings of experiences and convictions in the light of scriptural precedents. Once more, it must be acknowledged that Spong has latched on to an important insight; the similarity of some New Testament passages to the Jewish interpretive technique known as midrash is widely recognized. And Bishop Spong is not the first person to overuse a legitimate insight already abused by a well-known scholar (in this case Michael Goulder). In any case, for Spong, everything in the New Testament has now become midrash. This means in effect that Spong can proceed in his usual reductive manner, first to discredit the historicity of all New Testament accounts of the resurrection, and second, to provide his own version of "what really happened," all under the rubric of a legitimate (and impressive sounding) interpretive principle. In this case, we are told again that the resurrection turns out to be Simon Peter's dawning realization, some six months after the crucifixion, that God was at work in the life and death of Jesus, and, therefore, "death could not contain him."

Spong's argument is specious and his conclusion banal. His book is of interest mainly for the way in which it demonstrates the pattern I have been describing. We see again the ever-lengthening list of scholars invoked, the embrace of the spirit of modernity with its inability to stomach the miraculous, the claim at once that his conclusions will cause dismay among traditional believers yet represent what all enlightened people think anyhow, a claim that serves to make Spong more "honest" than his peers because he states openly what they think secretly. We observe Spong's regular detestation of the institutional church and its dogmas, and his connection of these to the right-wing politics he so obviously despises.

We see as well, however, a strange reluctance to lay aside the Scriptures. Though emptied of their literal content, they are affirmed in their symbolic significance. Yet when pressed for some specificity for the "symbol" of the resurrection, Spong can do little better than to affirm that it signifies insight into the special quality of Jesus' life. What that might mean once the particulars of Jesus' life have been consumed by criticism, Spong does not reveal. Finally, we see how the question of the historical Jesus is assumed to impinge on the question of Christianity's origins: the subtitle reads, "A Bishop's Search for the Origins of Christianity."

Bishop Spong's peculiar position in the cultural wars I am describing will need to be revisited, for he represents the perfect exemplification of the way in which the cultures of the church, of the academy, and of mass communication come together in unholy alliance. As Spong notes in his preface, "Most significantly, and beyond my wildest imagination, I have written the three books that have lifted me as an author onto both a national and international stage. . . . So it is that I find myself hated and feared by some and at the same time a kind of religious folk hero for others" (pp. xii–xiv). He is conscious that he exercises a kind of leadership, and is confident that he will have a successor: "I am certain that within that body there is already at this moment the one upon whom the mantle of this style of leadership will fall" (p. xiv). Quite apart from the grandiosity this sort of statement suggests, the puzzling thing about Spong is that he appears so blithely innocent concerning the "academic study of the Bible" he is so eager—as a bishop!—to import into the church, and so oblivious to the implications of his courtship of and by the mass media that has resulted in his being lifted "onto both a national and international stage."

A. N. WILSON

A. N. Wilson is a British novelist and biographer who turned from treatments of Milton, Belloc, Tolstoy, and C. S. Lewis to *Jesus* (W. W. Norton, 1992). He begins in by now predictable fashion by declaring that the dogmas of Christianity are just not believable anymore, at least not by him: "I did not feel it was honest to continue to call myself a Christian, to attend churches which addressed Jesus as if he were alive, to recite creeds which acknowledged Jesus as Lord and Judge of the world" (p. xvi). Like many before him, however, Wilson came to the conclusion that it was the hateful and hate-filled Paul of Tarsus who had invented the form of Christianity Wilson no longer found palatable. Jesus was not responsible for Christian origins. It wasn't his fault that he was regarded as divine.

With the breathlessness typical of such books, Wilson announces the academic resource that gives him access to Jesus the historical figure. Geza Vermeš's *Jesus the Jew* (1973) has provided Wilson with the key to discovering Jesus "as a recognizable Jew of the first century" (p. xvii). In Vermeš's construal, Jesus appears as a Galilean *chasid* or charismatic figure, like Honi the Circle Maker of rabbinic fame. Remarkably, Wilson immediately avers, ". . . this is the Jesus in whom I have come to believe." What it could possibly mean to "believe in" Jesus as an ancient charismatic wonder-worker is (perhaps fortunately) not spelled out.

Having dismissed the Christian confession of Jesus as a Pauline invention, Wilson is free to investigate Jesus as a historical figure, which he designates with disarming simplicity as "the real Jesus" (p. ix). But since he has from the start decided that Jesus' message can be summarized as "belief in God and Judaism" (p. 8), it is difficult to find in Jesus any distinguishing marks that should make him of interest. His resurrection is interpreted as a physical resuscitation and therefore considered as silly and not worth discussing further (p. 6). At the end of the book, Wilson is understandably left with some puzzlement concerning Jesus' impact: ". . . we can only be surprised that a historical figure of whom so little is known should have attracted to himself a reputation such as theology would wish to give him" (p. 230). Christian origins, Wilson seems to think, present an insoluble puzzle, once Jesus has been reduced to just another Jew and the resurrection to just another resuscitation. The only explanation left is an evil creative genius!

Wilson follows the familiar path of reduction: the surface problems of the text are used to create skepticism concerning their historical reliability. That accomplished, the way is open to speculation on what "really happened" on the author's terms, unconstrained by evidence (pp. 26–27). Wilson's own criterion of historicity might be called the "idiosyncratic aesthetic." In practice, this means "what strikes his fancy." Little is said about Jesus' teaching; the focus is on the story. Tiny details of the narratives that capture Wilson's attention (who knows why?)—such as the "cooked fish" of John's resurrection account—are used to reconstruct Wilson's version of Jesus' life. In effect, he skims through the narratives, correcting this point or that, making connections on the basis of nothing much more than oddity or what he considers psychological plausibility. Thus, Wilson has convinced himself that Paul had to have known Jesus personally, so he works him into the plot by identifying him with the Malchus of the arrest scene. Likewise, the key to the Last Supper account is the "Man with the Pitcher," whom Wilson regards as a symbol of Aquarius and therefore a portent of the messianic age—since Jesus was "probably no exception" to the Essene interest in astrology as shown, he alleges, by the Qumran scrolls! And much more of the same.

Having discredited Christian dogma, the apostle Paul, and the reliability of the Gospel narratives, Wilson is content to have found a Jesus he can live with: "I have found that in seeking him as a historical being, he has been in some ways much more vivid to me than he ever was when I tried to approach him through the eyes of Christian belief" (p. xvii). The self-administered therapy has worked: the threatening Christ of faith has been replaced by a harmless Jew of the first century. We are meant to feel relieved.

STEPHEN MITCHELL

Another attempt to rescue the "real Jesus" from the clutches of benighted dogma is Stephen Mitchell's *The Gospel According to Jesus* (HarperCollins, 1991), which is subtitled, "A New Translation and Guide to His Essential Teachings for Believers and Unbelievers." Mitchell consciously places himself in continuity with Thomas Jefferson's *The Life and Morals of Jesus of Nazareth*, which sought to distill the essential Jesus from "the corruptions of Christianity." These include all the unattractive bits—mainly Jesus' harsher sayings (p. 8)—and all the "legends" attached to Jesus' birth, death, resurrection, and special titles (p. 18); all the elements, in short, that make Jesus distinctive if not unique. Mitchell considers the story of Jesus irrelevant, anyway: "Jesus has left the essence of himself in his teachings, which are all we need to know about him" (p. 16).

But of all the teachings in the Gospels, how do we know which ones really represent Jesus' "essence"? Mitchell makes the mandatory bow to "scholarly criteria" for determining authentic sayings (p. 6) but relies more on his own sense of fitness, what he and Jefferson consider to be Jesus' "sublime ideas" (p. 7). Anything that smacks of "later theological or polemical or legendary accretion" must therefore be tossed out, leaving a residue of sayings that have obvious "spiritual value" (p. 6). Once this is accomplished, Jesus can be seen to speak "in harmony with the supreme teachings of all the great religions" (p. 9), by which Mitchell apparently means the mystical streams within world religions: Jesus "is a man who has emptied himself of desires, doctrines, rules—all the mental claptrap and spiritual baggage that separates us from true life—and has been filled with the vital reality of the unnameable" (p. 13).

Jesus' entire gospel consists of this: "The love we all long for in our innermost heart is already present, beyond longing." Or, more simply still: "Jesus taught one thing only: presence." It is noteworthy that Mitchell provides no textual reference in support of this gospel summation. In fact, none is available. As for Jesus' proclamation of the kingdom of God, he meant "a state of being, a way of living at ease among the joys and sorrows of *our* world"; it is "feeling, as if we were floating in the womb of the universe, that we are being taken care of at every moment" (p. 12). In short, Jesus is "like a mirror for us all, showing us who we essentially are" (p. 14).

It may be difficult for other readers to find in the actual words of the Gospels anything corresponding to this image of Jesus as one who advocates "living at ease" and "floating in the womb of the universe," for none of the sayings attributed to him in the Gospels actually comes close to saying these things. In fact, Mitchell's book is a wonderfully transparent exercise in finding the Jesus one sets out to find, a Jesus according to one's own image of who a teacher should be, to provide a "mirror for ourselves." At least he is straightforward about it.

And Mitchell's account is not without charm. He performs an intricate and plausible psychological "reading" of Jesus' experience as an illegitimate child whose discovery of a God whom he could designate as *Abba* was a breakthrough spiritual enlightenment and a key to his troubled relations with his family (pp. 29–54). He also manages to connect Jesus' teaching on forgiveness with his own psychological history. What he somehow fails to realize, however, is that such a reconstruction depends heavily on precisely those parts of the story that he has already dismissed as "legendary." Such inconsistency is to be expected in the amateur, but we will meet it repeatedly in the experts as well.

Enter the Academicians

Among those eager to reform Christianity on the basis of a reconstructed Jesus are full-fledged members of the biblical guild. I turn now to three genuine academicians whose books on Jesus and Christian origins have figured prominently in the recent controversy. What is most striking about these books, however, is that beneath the academic polish, the same pattern persists.

MARCUS BORG

Marcus Borg is an example of a member of the Jesus Seminar who was not removed from his position for his views, and in fact made considerable progress in his academic career through the production of a series of books on the Historical Jesus. He is now Hundere Professor of Religion and Culture in the Department of Philosophy at Oregon State University, and by his own account has been researching Jesus for some twenty years. His recent book, *Meeting Jesus Again for the First Time: The Historical Jesus and the Heart of Contemporary Faith* (HarperSanFrancisco, 1994), is basically a reworking of his earlier production, *Jesus, A New Vision: Spirit, Culture, and the Life of Discipleship* (Harper & Row, San Francisco, 1987). The main difference is that the second book is even more explicitly directed to the reformation of Christian faith on the basis of history. The lessons derived by Borg from the historical Jesus are applied without mediation to "the life of faith." As the subtitles indicate, however, both books are clearly directed to the reshaping of Christian perceptions of Jesus and therefore of faith itself. More recently still, he has come out with *Jesus in Contemporary Scholarship* (Trinity Press International, 1994), whose basic approach remains virtually identical to the first book mentioned here, containing, so far as I can tell, no substantively new data or argument. My attention therefore is directed primarily to *Jesus, A New Vision*.

Borg declares his intention in the preface to *Jesus, A New Vision* to be one of making accessible to the general reader "a synopsis of modern Jesus scholarship," while at the same time advancing his own modification of the "dominant scholarly image" of Jesus. His motivation is to enable readers to "see some of Jesus' significance for our time." Borg declares an allegiance to the Christianity in which he was raised, although for a long time he was, in his words, "an unbelieving son of the church." The research he did into the historical Jesus apparently had the effect of restimulating Borg's faith. Borg wants to share his enthusiasm.

The "popular image of Jesus," by which Borg means the traditional understanding of Jesus in Christianity, pictures Jesus as a "divine or semi-divine figure." Sadly, he declares, this will no longer serve (p. 2). It has roots in the New Testament, to be sure (p. 3), but it is an image fundamentally at odds with "what Jesus was like as a figure of history before his death" (p. 4). Borg subscribes, then, to a second image of Jesus developed by critical scholarship, since "the image of the historical Jesus as a divine or semi-divine figure, who saw himself as the divine savior whose purpose was to die for the sins of the world, and whose message consisted in preaching that, is simply not historically true" (p. 7). We can leave aside for the moment the fairness of that summary. The important thing for Borg is that "scholarship" has disqualified the image of Jesus held by traditional faith.

But Borg also disagrees with what he calls the "dominant scholarly image" of Jesus that bases itself on his proclamation of the kingdom of God. This image is of an eschatological prophet (p. 10). Borg asserts, with some justification, that "the two dominant currents of twentieth-century scholarship on Jesus—historical skepticism and eschatological emphasis—have made the historical Jesus seem irrelevant" (p. 13). That the historical Jesus should be without relevance to Christian faith is unthinkable for Borg (p. 14). And it is precisely with the intention of making Jesus relevant to Christianity that Borg develops his "third image" of Jesus, that of "a charismatic, who was a healer, sage, prophet, and revitalization movement founder" (p. 15). He tries to show that it is precisely in Jesus' religious experience and in his cultural interactions that Jesus regains his significance: "to follow Jesus means in some sense to be 'like him,' to take seriously what he took seriously," which can provide us with "an alternative vision of life" (p. 17).

There are, however, a number of things here that are puzzling. The first is Borg's desire to be both a critical historian and a builder of Christian faith, or, better, to build faith through critical history. If Borg is a Christian who believes that the risen Christ "does share all of the qualities of God," why should it matter to him if "the historical Jesus did not" and the New Testament retrojected "divine qualities back onto Jesus" (p. 7)? If Jesus is, by virtue of his resurrection, powerfully alive in God, how does the retrojection of that understanding distort "the real Jesus"? Conversely, if he is a critical historian, why should he worry whether the historical Jesus is "irrelevant to the faith" (p. 14)? The second odd thing is Borg's apparent assumption that "the human vision" of Jesus is somehow to be the norm for "the new vision" that shapes Christian discipleship.

Before turning to Borg's reconstruction and how it should speak to Christians, it is worth pausing over the quality of the "critical scholarship" on which his argument is based. Borg vigorously rejects the notion that Jesus was an "eschatological prophet." But on what basis? First, Borg equates "eschatological" with the belief that the end of the world is imminent. This is obviously a simplification of a complex set of beliefs about "the end-time." Next, Borg in 1986 conducted a mail poll of seventy-two scholars associated with the Jesus Seminar and with the Historical Jesus section of the Society of Biblical Literature. The combined response indicated that 59 percent of those questioned thought "that Jesus did not expect the end of the world in his generation." The results of a direct poll of thirty-nine members of the Jesus Seminar in 1986? Thirty thought that Jesus did not expect the end of the world in his generation (p. 20, n. 25). We are not informed what the response might have been if "eschatological" had been defined more broadly—for example, "Did Jesus use language about the kingdom of God as a future reality?" No matter: on the basis of the *vote* of a self-selected group of like-minded scholars (at most, seventy out of the 6,900 members of the Society of Biblical Literature), Borg declares the issue settled: Jesus the eschatological prophet is out;

Jesus the countercultural sage is in. In *Jesus in Contemporary Scholarship* Borg offers a slightly different version of the polling results (pp. 59–61) and allows that the question of eschatology might require some expansion, but his basic position remains the same.

One of the striking features of Borg's "historical analysis" is how little real history is in it. But this, too, is deliberate, for "the present quest seeks to broaden the somewhat narrow focus on literary and historical method that has marked traditional scholarship" (p. 15). Borg therefore embraces "the social sciences, anthropology, and history of religions" as ways of refining the search for the historical Jesus. What *pesher* did for Thiering, and midrash did for Spong, the social sciences will provide for Borg and Crossan, namely, a way of unlocking the "real history" within the texts. In practice, however, the use of social sciences in Borg's book means the invocation of cultural parallels and analogies that are sometimes suggestive but rarely probative. Indeed, for a book that makes such sweeping claims, there is little real argument or exposition of texts. Much is asserted, little demonstrated.

To support his position that Jesus was a charismatic figure, for example, Borg relies heavily on Geza Vermeš's *Jesus the Jew,* which places Jesus in the category of Chanina Ben Dosa and Honi the Circle Maker as a "Galilean Hasid" (compare the use of Vermeš also by A. N. Wilson). The first problem with such an appropriation, however, is that the historical evidence for these two figures is far slenderer than that for Jesus, and just as difficult to disentangle from the ideological proclivities of the rabbinic tradition. Even if the traditions (very few in number) attaching to them were utterly reliable, furthermore, it is highly debatable whether two such figures can stand as evidence for a presumedly well-established religious type called the "charismatic *chasid*." The second problem is that Jesus' own religious experience is made to fit within that predetermined mold. Borg sees Jesus as a Spirit-defined person: "Jesus' vivid experience of Spirit radically challenges our culture's way of seeing reality" (p. 34). But if his experience was fundamentally the same as Honi's, why should it challenge our culture any more profoundly than Honi's Spirit experience does? Would not any charismatic figure fit the role Borg assigns to Jesus? Why should "Jesus' vision" have any influence on people after him?

In some ways, Borg's portrayal of Jesus is attractive. He is willing, for example, to acknowledge Jesus' activity as a healer and sage. But it is Jesus as prophet and founder of a renewal movement within Judaism that Borg finds most compelling and relevant. He understands Jesus' ministry as a kind of cultural critique of the "politics of holiness" that represented the conventional wisdom of first-century Judaism—religious concern for requirements on matters of diet and purity—and its replacement by a "politics of compassion." The politics of holiness, he asserts, is about law and status and exclusion, whereas the politics of compassion is about freedom and equality and inclusion (pp. 97–171). This prophetic counterculturalism got Jesus into trouble with the authorities, who did not want their status-conscious world threatened. Some Jewish leaders may consequently have been involved in Jesus' death, but the main responsibility lay with the Romans. For Borg, however, the real question is not *who* killed Jesus but rather *what* killed Jesus. The answer? "It was the conventional wisdom of the time—the 'dominant consciousness' of the day—that was responsible for the death of Jesus" (p. 182). As for Jesus' resurrection, it demonstrated that "Spirit triumphed over culture" (p. 185).

It does not take an exceptionally discerning eye to detect more than a little of the "dominant consciousness" of yet another sort at work in this analysis, namely, the cultural assumptions of the contemporary American academy. Jesus' "relevance" turns out to be the way in which he can function as the prototype of the sort of "cultural critique" that many academics think the rest of the world needs: the "politics of holiness" that is overly concerned with rules and status and exclusion should be replaced by a "politics of compassion" that is committed to freedom and equality and inclusion.

Borg's complaint that "the most common fruit of biblical scholarship in the [twentieth] century" has been its failure to provide a compelling image of Jesus is not without justice (p. 200). But the version he offers is ultimately platitudinous, the mirror reflection of Borg's own social location in the liberal academy. Neither John the Baptist nor Jesus has anything eschatological about him (p. 41). Jesus' proclamation of the kingdom of God is collapsed into a "politics of compassion" and "life in the Spirit" (pp. 197–98). But what Spirit? Jesus teaches nothing about God or about God's demands for life in the kingdom. Perhaps that is why Borg gives only one paragraph to Jesus' parables, for it is difficult to consider them without considering the embarrassing subjects of a coming kingdom and God.

Jesus apparently had nothing to say about judgment for sin or the forgiveness of sin. In Borg's subject index, the only entry under "sinner" is, revealingly, a cross-reference to "outcasts." The "politics of compassion," it seems, regards human beings as basically good: social structures are what corrupt and enslave them. But Jesus also had little to say about Torah or its interpretation (pp. 97–98). This is not so surprising, since Borg has claimed that the "politics of holiness" had its roots in the "conventional wisdom" of Torah (p. 82). But isn't this the very "politics of holiness" whose critique defines Jesus' ministry? In effect, despite Borg's effort to locate Jesus within Jewish culture, he has removed him from his Jewishness entirely. Palestinian Judaism serves the function of providing a stereotyped foil to Jesus. Jesus' mission—in new code and with politically correct language—emerges as an updated version of the second-century teacher Marcion (see chapter 6), who worked with the same contrast: harsh and judgmental Judaism is replaced by a compassionate and liberating Jesus!

JOHN DOMINIC CROSSAN

One of the most impressive and imposing of the recent books on the historical Jesus comes from another charter member and co-chair of the Jesus Seminar, whose research has preceded and progressed well beyond that of his colleagues in that association. John Dominic Crossan began working on the parables as an avenue to the historical Jesus in his *In Parables* (1973), then expanded his analysis to noncanonical sources (*Four Other Gospels: Shadows on the Contours of the Canon*, 1985; *The Cross That Spoke: The Origins of the Passion Narrative*, 1988), and finally combined source analysis with an approach to the figure of Jesus within first-century Judaism that is heavily influenced by cultural anthropology. His major and widely publicized *The Historical Jesus: The Life of a Mediterranean Jewish Peasant* (HarperSanFrancisco, 1991) was followed quickly by an abbreviated version, *Jesus: A Revolutionary Biography* (HarperSanFrancisco, 1994), then a stripped-down version of the authentic sayings of Jesus called *The Essential Jesus* (HarperSanFrancisco, 1994), and finally *Who Killed Jesus? Exposing the Roots of Anti-Semitism in the Gospel*

Story of the Death of Jesus (HarperSanFrancisco, 1995). My comments will focus primarily on his fullest study, *The Historical Jesus*.

More than any of the authors so far discussed, Crossan shows consistent commitment to certain methodological procedures. Like others in his circle, Crossan considers the sayings of Jesus found in extracanonical gospels (particularly the *Gospel of Thomas*) as of equal or even greater value than the canonical Gospels for reconstructing the teaching of Jesus. He employs an elaborate system of stratification for the Jesus traditions, confident that the criteria he employs enable him to detect not only the earliest traditions but also the various stages of development that subsequently are built upon them. *The Historical Jesus* opens with a complete selection of "the Gospel according to Jesus," a gathering of the sayings that Crossan considers Jesus' own. This collection he calls a "score to be played and a program to be enacted" (pp. xiii–xxvi; see also *The Essential Jesus*). Like his succinct discussion of his social-scientific and textual stratification strategies (pp. xxvii–xxxiv), this opening ploy suggests Crossan's overall approach to his subject.

He takes it as self-evident that Gospel criticism has denied us the possibility of tracing Jesus' actions in sequence. But he is confident that we can winnow out Jesus' characteristic deeds and sayings. By placing those deeds and sayings within the social-historical context reconstructed with the help of ancient extra-Christian sources and a healthy dose of cross-cultural theories, we can begin to approximate and appreciate the character of Jesus' brief active mission.

Crossan's book unfolds according to the parts of its subtitle, "The Life of a Mediterranean Jewish Peasant." He examines the context of Greco-Roman culture under the rubric of "The Brokered Empire" (pp. 1–88), using cross-cultural studies to define the first-century Mediterranean world as an empire with a stratified system of patronage operating within a symbolic framework of honor and shame. Then, in "Embattled Brokerage," he tries to show what it would have meant to be a "Jewish peasant" in first-century Palestine. Here, he is heavily dependent on the work of Richard Horsely and others, who portray that world in terms of responses to oppressive Roman occupation: the cooperation of turncoats like Josephus, the sporadic resistance of peasant strikes and rural banditry, the militant resistance shown by the radical revolutionaries.

Although these impressively drawn descriptions of the Greco-Roman and Jewish worlds make up fully half of his study, such a thick description is critical to his method, for the framework provides the essential shape into which the various "authentic Jesus pieces" can be placed.

Crossan describes Jesus' ministry under the rubric of "The Brokerless Kingdom." Jesus began by sharing John the Baptist's apocalyptic outlook, but his own ministry took on an increasingly sapiential rather than apocalyptic character (p. 259). At the heart of Crossan's depiction of Jesus is his analysis of "Kingdom and Wisdom" (pp. 265–302). He critically sifts through Jesus' parables and sayings to show how Jesus understood the kingdom to be made up of such "nobodies" of the world as children, the outcast, and the poor. In effect, Jesus enunciates a vision of countercultural egalitarianism that, in Crossan's view, most resembles that of the ancient Cynic philosophers. Indeed, his epilogue refers to Jesus as a "Peasant Jewish Cynic" (p. 421).

Crossan considers the chapter entitled "Magic and Meal" (pp. 303–53) to be "possibly the key chapter in the book" (p. xxix). In it, he examines the traditions dealing with Jesus' healings and exorcisms. Not only does he tend to give considerable credit to the authenticity of such traditions in general, he finds that the actions of Jesus support the vision sketched by his words. In Jesus' sending out of delegates during his lifetime, Crossan finds the extension of Jesus' open table fellowship in a program of peasant freelance thaumaturgy and solidarity that would inevitably prove provocative to an elite structured in terms of temple prerogatives and the privileges of exclusivism. Jesus' "kingdom" is, in short, a "style of life" that enables all access to fellowship and wisdom without the "brokerage" of social status and patronage. As in Borg's *Jesus, A New Vision*, Jesus' ministry turns out fundamentally to be a social critique of established structure and hierarchical power. Crossan's peasant Cynic who preaches inclusiveness and equality fits perfectly within the idealized ethos of the late-twentieth-century academic: he is nonpatriarchal and noninstitutional; his kingdom consists of an open table where everyone accepts everyone else.

Crossan is a gifted writer who carries his readers along so brilliantly that some effort is required to tear one's eyes away from his reconstruction and assess more carefully his ways of reaching it and its implications. At first, for example, Crossan's insistence that all Jesus traditions—from apocryphal as well as canonical writings—must be put on an even footing appears as simple fair-mindedness and intellectual rigor: he will demand that every strand of tradition prove itself! But closer examination suggests that the game is fixed. Crossan's remarkably early dating for virtually all apocryphal materials, and his correspondingly late dating for virtually all canonical materials, together with his frequent assertion that the extracanonical sources are unaffected by the canonical sources and therefore have independent evidenciary value, rests on little more than his assertions and those of the like-minded colleagues he cites. He never enters into debate with those who do *not* share such views. The position, in other words, is presumed, not proved.

By placing all the individual pieces into competition, furthermore, Crossan has actually freed himself to establish his own lines of dependence and development. He makes judgments on such matters so frequently and with such confidence that the lack of real controls is camouflaged and the circularity of his method is easily missed. Crossan cunningly combines impressive heaps of data with an air of utter reasonableness. If the reader has no way of challenging his selection of data, or his way of arranging it, Crossan's conclusions appear not only reasonable but right.

His bias against canonical materials in favor of apocryphal ones, clear enough in his discussion of Jesus' ministry, becomes flagrant in his discussion of Jesus' death (pp. 354–94). Like Borg, Crossan experiences some difficulty in connecting his account of Jesus' ministry with his death. The ministry is understood as a challenge to the "brokerage of the kingdom" exercised by the temple cult, priesthood, and Jewish leadership. Yet Crossan is uneasy about attributing Jesus' death to such Jewish authorities. The Romans must be held responsible. The provocative character of Jesus' ministry as a whole and the prophetic challenge represented by his gesture in the Temple are therefore curiously left inconclusive.

Crossan's discussion of Jesus' death is flawed most, however, by his source theories. He spends an inordinate amount of effort trying to demonstrate the dependence of all the passion accounts on an early edition of the apocryphal *Gospel of Peter*. The reader begins to suspect that such textual prestidigitation must stem from a commitment to consider *any* source outside the canon as more reliable than a source inside the canon, and that something more than a desire for sober historical reconstruction is at work. The same sense is given by Crossan's odd insistence on "the dogs beneath the cross"— that Jesus was not buried but left abandoned to be eaten by scavenging animals—as emblematic of the finality and insignificance of Jesus' death in *Jesus: A Revolutionary Biography* (pp. 123–28). Crossan's most recent book (*Who Killed Jesus?*), in fact, is a defense of his own conclusion that the passion of Jesus is "prophecy historicized" through an elaborate process of scribal activity, rather than "history remembered." This book is noteworthy for its sustained debate with R. E. Brown's *The Death of the Messiah: From Gethsemane to the Grave. A Commentary on the Passion Narratives in the Four Gospels* (Doubleday, 1994) concerning the role of the Jews in the death of Jesus. But it is most of all a defense of his own conviction that the apocryphal *Gospel of Peter* is the key to the development of the passion accounts.

Crossan's discussion of the resurrection is equally bland, in contrast to his vivid depiction of Jesus' ministry (pp. 395–416). Once more, he gives more credit to the deeply suspect *Secret Gospel of Mark* than he does to the canonical sources. Even more revealingly, he analyzes the appearance accounts exclusively in terms of the way in which they legitimated authority in the early church: the chapter is entitled, "Resurrection and Authority." The implication is plain: as soon as there was a church, there was no longer a "brokerless kingdom," but one brokered by a new system of authority. This reading of the resurrection, it should be noted, is if anything made even stronger in *Who Killed Jesus?* (pp. 202–8).

Indeed, Crossan is fairly clear about the theological agenda underlying his historical portrayal. He acknowledges that historical reconstructions are always just that, reconstructions (*Jesus*, p. 199), and that there is always a dialectic between a "historically read Jesus and a theologically read Christ" (*Historical Jesus*, p. 423). But he closes his major book with this flat statement: "If you cannot believe in something produced by reconstruction, you may have nothing left to believe in" (*Historical Jesus*, p. 426). And in *Jesus*, he declares that all Christian belief is (1) an act of faith (2) in the historical Jesus (3) as the manifestation of God (p. 200). This is a remarkable enough claim, and one necessary to question further later. But it makes intelligible the specific reformist thrust of his work. Crossan "the historian" has a theological agenda: his reconstructed Jesus is to provide a vision of Christian faith that should overturn that of the Constantinian era (read: established Christianity). He states in *Who Killed Jesus?* that "It is not (in a postmodern world) that we find once and for all who the historical Jesus was way back then. It is that each generation and century must redo that historical work and establish its best reconstruction, a reconstruction that will be and must be in some creative tension with its own particular needs, visions, and programs . . . it is that Jesus reconstructed in the dialogues, debates, controversies, and *conclusions of contemporary scholarship* that *challenges faith* to see and say how that is *for now* the Christ, the Lord, the Son of God" (p. 217; emphasis added). We recognize in this statement the precise agenda enunciated by Funk for the Jesus Seminar.

Crossan desires Christianity to return to the vision of a "brokerless kingdom." The paradox is that the key to this vision—the historical Jesus—is precisely the "broker" whom Christianity must reject if it is to truly live by his vision.

Even as Crossan's theological agenda becomes clearer in his two books on the historical Jesus, the actual character of his historical reconstruction grows more puzzling. Jesus is so much collapsed into the stereotype of "the peasant" that he loses not only his uniqueness but even any distinctiveness as a human person. This Jesus, once more, is the embodiment of a cultural critique, more than a specific historical person. Nothing in his reconstructed mission, furthermore, seems to have a specifically religious character: once more, we see in this Jesus no interpretation of Torah; nothing of the judgment or forgiveness of sins; virtually no talk about God; and certainly no declarations concerning a sense of mission with regard to the Jewish people as God's people.

Crossan does not seem to realize that by confining Jesus' possibilities to those available to his (theoretical) construct of a peasant, he only increases the *historical* implausibility of his own reconstruction. If Jesus' open commensality did not have a specifically religious character or claim God's will as its justification, why should the religious establishment have worried about it? And if the religious establishment of Judaism did not actively participate in his demise, it is even harder to figure out how a program so utopian yet bland as that attributed to this peasant might appear to the Roman authorities as a threat to their brokered empire. Again, if Jesus' death was the sort of "accidental occasion" that the oppressive Roman rule might carry out on any odd day, then why should it have been remembered at all? If the resurrection appearance accounts are mere legitimations for the authority of leaders within the movement, how do we account for the rise of the movement in the first place? Why should there even *be* a scribal follower of Jesus five years after so obscure a death who would want to interpret it through a midrashic reading of Scripture (see *Historical Jesus*, pp. 376–83)?

For all their self-conscious methodology and social-scientific sophistication, Crossan's efforts reveal themselves as an only slightly camouflaged exercise in theological revisionism rather than genuine historiography. Crossan pays virtually no attention to the light that might be shed on "the historical Jesus" by references, for example, in Paul. His accounts of Christian origins bypass completely those in canonical writings such as the Acts of the Apostles. To construct his portrayal of Jesus, he will draw on any apocryphal writing in preference to any canonical writing. The criteria that matter for determining authenticity are those that make up the predetermined portrait that Crossan wishes to emerge. His use of cross-cultural patterns reduces Jesus to a stereotyped cultural category, that of a member of "peasant culture." Into this *historical cipher* Crossan can pour his own vision of what "Christianity" ought to be: not a church with leaders and cult and creeds, but a loose association of Cynic philosophers who broker their own access to the kingdom of self-esteem and mutual acceptance.

BURTON MACK

A final book to consider in this survey of publications relating to the new quest for the historical Jesus is Burton Mack's *The Lost Gospel: The Book of Q and Christian Origins* (HarperSanFrancisco, 1993). Even though it does not directly take up the question of the historical Jesus, Mack's entire project assumes the sort of approach to Jesus found in Borg and Crossan, and illustrates even more clearly the way "Jesus research" connects to the question of Christian origins and to a theological agenda fundamentally hostile to traditional Christianity.

The Lost Gospel extends and popularizes some themes found in Mack's earlier and much larger book, *A Myth of Innocence: Mark and Christian Origins* (Fortress, 1988). In that publication, he presents Jesus in the form now familiar to us from our review of Borg and Crossan. Jesus is a wisdom teacher of the Cynic sort. It is important to Mack that Jesus' work took place primarily in Galilee, for that territory was thoroughly hellenized and less "Jewish." But it is even more important to assert that Jesus was primarily a teacher who set in motion a "social experiment," without anything divine, salvific, or, apparently, even very distinctive about it (*Myth,* pp. 53–97). Only after Jesus' death, for reasons Mack cannot explain, do these movements take on a cultic coloration in some areas (*Myth,* pp. 98–131).

Mack's basic premise, then, is that there is no "big bang" at the origin of Christianity—no heroic Jesus and certainly no resurrection experience. Instead, Mack assumes the independent birth of movements and cults loosely associated with Jesus or "the Christ." Only slowly did these movements create a "myth of origins" connected to Jesus, in which his "historical" career as a Cynic sage was reread in terms of divine power. For Mack, Mark's Gospel is the fundamental defining document of "Christianity." It is also, in his eyes, a terrible mistake, and a fall from grace.

In *The Lost Gospel,* Mack proposes to trace the "history" of an important segment of the Jesus movement in Galilee (and therefore closely connected to Jesus himself!) by revealing the development of traditions within what he calls "The Lost Gospel." The title itself is intentionally sensational, suggesting as it does the sort of out-from-secrecy breathlessness that accompanied the discovery of the "Gnostic gospels." But in fact, Mack has simply chosen to *treat* as a separate "gospel" a certain body of material within the canonical Gospels. Specifically, he is dealing with the material found in both Matthew and Luke but absent from Mark. Scholars working on the synoptic problem (the literary relationships among Matthew, Mark, and Luke) had long recognized the distinctiveness of this material, whose thematic and linguistic resemblances suggest that Matthew and Luke were using a separate written source in addition to Mark. This source was identified simply as Q (for the German *Quelle,* "source").

Scholars were, however, cautious concerning Q. Indeed, a small but vocal minority of scholars deny the "Q hypothesis" entirely, thinking that the relationships among the synoptic Gospels can better be accounted for by the direct use of Matthew by Luke, and the use of both Luke and Matthew by Mark. In such a view, no "second source" such as Q need be hypothesized. But even scholars convinced that Q is a necessary hypothesis tended to a benign agnosticism concerning its precise dimensions or provenance. All we knew of it, after all, was the form it took in the two editions of Matthew and Luke. Determining what the original source looked like in all its particulars was impossible: we did not know where it began or where it ended; nor could we tell in each instance whether Luke's version or Matthew's was closer to the "original."

But in recent years, some scholars (such as Helmut Koester, James Robinson, Richard Edwards, and John Kloppenborg) pushed past such resistance to treat Q as if it were a specific, determinable composition rather than a convenient designation for a body of shared material. Many other scholars have taken up the chase, and there is even a Q Seminar of the Society of Biblical Literature that combs through these verses in search of redactional layers and other arcana.

Now Mack takes Q as a "Lost Gospel" and seeks to find in it the "history" of a community associated with the Jesus movement somewhere in Galilee over a period of some thirty years after the death of Jesus. Indeed, he claims to trace the *development* of that community structurally and ideologically, as it moves from a loose table fellowship that traded Jesus quips as an expression of countercultural consciousness and collegiality, to an increasingly beleaguered and apocalyptic sectarian claimant to the heritage of Israel.

As we follow his argument, we need to remind ourselves that Mack presents himself as the soberest of historians. No flight to faith, no theological fantasies. But what are the assumptions the reader must accept at the various stages? First, the material found in Matthew and Luke but not in Mark comes from the same source; that is, these diverse sayings came not from several compositions but from one. Second, what we now have from that source is all it ever contained; this is critical, for if it had other material in it that we don't now have, then that would naturally affect our analysis of it. Third, the original form of the composition can be recovered by omitting the alterations and emendations made by Matthew and Luke when they used it as a source. Fourth, the document thus reconstituted contains the sole literature of a specific social movement—its members read nothing else and held no other beliefs than those contained in this single writing. Fifth, it is possible to demarcate *stages* in the redaction of Q according to the principles of literary analysis. Sixth, these stages are thematically self-enclosed: there is no connection between the Cynic-type sayings in Q1 and the rules and rejection motifs found in Q2 or the apocalyptic mythologization in Q3. Seventh, these stages of redaction correspond *exactly* to stages in the hypothetical community's social "development."

These are a great many assumptions to demand. But Mack asks still another of the reader: that this group was an early form of the "Jesus movement" untouched and uninfluenced by the "Jerusalem Church" or the Pauline "Christ Cult." So mesmerizing is this progression, and so similar to the procedures carried out by other scholars to less dramatic conclusions, that only upon reflection does it become clear that the entire argument is pure flimflam. There is no positive evidence for a community of this character in Galilee. Mack has based his entire argument on a set of arbitrary assumptions concerning the way texts and communities work. If the "Q Community" read anything besides "Q," Mack's argument is invalidated—even if we were to grant *all* the other premises! Mack also requires of us that we ignore all the evidence provided by other canonical writings (especially the Acts of the Apostles and Paul's letters) concerning earliest Christianity. Most of all, Mack leaves us with the question left also by Borg and Crossan. If there was no impressive "founder" and no real "founding experience," then how do we account for such a proliferation of movements and such a production of literature "in this name"? The historical question of origination is not answered, only avoided.

It is very unlikely, however, that Mack is really interested in history. At the end of *Myth of Innocence,* Mack turned to what he considered the disastrous consequences of Mark's Gospel: Mark's making Jesus the founder of Christianity was the first step on the road to everything bad in Christianity and then in Western culture, down to the genocide of Native Americans, Star Wars, and Reaganomics (pp. 353–76). Now, in the epilogue to *Lost Gospel,* he offers the antidote. Note these three sentences: "Q's challenge strikes to the heart of the traditional understanding of Christian Origins.". . . "Q is the best record we have for the first forty years of the Jesus movements.". . . "The question now is whether the discovery of Q has any chance of making a difference in the way in which Christianity and its gospel are viewed in modern times" (pp. 245–47). Mack sees no trouble in moving directly from the descriptive to the normative. He declares that Christians can no longer privilege the narrative Gospels of the canon, since they "are also products of mythic imagination" (p. 250). Mack wants Q to help in "breaking the taboo that now grants privilege to the Christian Myth" in American culture (p. 254). In short, just as Q represented a leaderless group of cultural critics in an imaginary Galilee of the past, so should Christians today "make some contribution to the urgent task of cultural critique where it seems to matter most—understanding the social consequences of Christian Mythology" (p. 258). Meager history reveals itself as thin theology.

Constant Traits

Although differing greatly in style and in quality of scholarship, these books on the historical Jesus share certain consistent features:

1. To a remarkable extent, they reject the canonical Gospels as reliable sources for our knowledge of Jesus. The New Testament Gospels must be purified of "later accretions" or the "distortions of faith," or they must be put in competition with apocryphal gospels, or a more important source must be excavated from within them, or they must be read as an elaborate allegory. In short, if the "real Jesus" is to be found, he must be found somewhere other than in the Gospels as they are read by Christians.

2. To an equal degree, these books shape their portrait of Jesus and their account of Christian origins without reference to other canonical sources. Paul's letters are in particular regarded as irrelevant for historical knowledge about Jesus, since Paul is regarded, in one way or another, as the "inventor" or at least the champion of the "Christ cult" that so many of these authors deem the first step toward the distortion of the "Jesus movement."

3. The mission of Jesus and the Jesus movement are portrayed in terms of a social or cultural critique rather than in terms of religious or spiritual reali-

ties. Although credit may be given to Jesus as a charismatic figure, he is not fundamentally defined in terms of religious experience and conviction. His location in Judaism is largely one of criticism of its "politics of holiness" (Borg). The Jesus movement, likewise, is fundamentally a cultural critique; when it becomes "Christianity," it is already in decline.

4. Although these books have all committed themselves to the "historical Jesus," they all reveal themselves to have as well a theological agenda. They state in one way or another that traditional Christian belief is a distortion of the "real Jesus" and that institutional Christianity is a distortion of the "Jesus movement." In Crossan and Mack, moreover, the destructive aspects of traditional Christianity are rooted not only in its creed, but specifically in the *narratives* of the canonical Gospels themselves. They clearly want their understanding of Jesus and Christian origins to have an impact on Christianity, primarily by removing "the privilege of Christian Myth" (Mack).

5. Whether implicit or explicit, the shared premise of these books is that *historical knowledge* is normative for faith, and therefore for theology. This is perhaps stated most explicitly by Crossan, "If you cannot believe in something produced by reconstruction, you may have nothing left to believe in." In addition, there is the assumption that *origins* define *essence:* the first understanding of Jesus was necessarily better than any following; the original form of the Jesus movement was naturally better than any of its developments. Such epistemological premises underlie the implication that a new vision of "the real Jesus" should automatically send Christians to check their creed.

6. One would think that such a critical agenda—a demand for the dismantling of traditional Christian views—would come from outsiders, perhaps Christianity's cultured despisers. But such is not the case. The only real outsider among these authors is Stephen Mitchell, who seeks to rescue from the gospel and Christian faith a Jesus more in tune with universal religious aspirations. All the rest, in varying degrees, have some form of identification with Christianity. This commitment, however, is less strong than that professed toward scholarship. If there is a "church" whose rules and rituals are home to these authors, it is that of the academy. The ideals espoused in this "church" provide the perspective for the criticism of the Christian "Church," which in all these discussions appears only as a problem and never as a mystery, always as

a tragic mistake and never as a providential development. The most startling figure in terms of social location is Bishop Spong, whose adopted academic identity provides the legitimation for his sustained attack on the beliefs of the communion he purportedly serves as an official leader and teacher. At the same time, it is his position within the church that gives his unoriginal and derivative form of "scholarship" its visibility and notoriety, and, in his words, "lifted me as an author onto both a national and international stage." Bishop Spong, in short, is great press.

The interconnections of two cultural institutions, the church and the academy, have been touched on in this preliminary review of the Jesus Seminar and recent Historical Jesus books. In the next chapter, the issue of "culture war" needs to be considered more closely: what is really happening within the academy and the church as they play out this struggle between history and faith in and through the media? Only after facing that issue can we turn to a more substantive reflection on the links between faith and history, and between history and theology.

CHAPTER 3

Cultural Confusion and Collusion

My review of recent scholarship and media coverage identifies two sets of sharply differing perceptions concerning Jesus, the Christian religion, the Church, and the New Testament. On one side is the perception of Jesus given by the Christian creed: Jesus is declared as Son of God. The significance of Jesus is not determined by his ministry alone, but above all and essentially by the mystery of his death and resurrection. For the Christian confession, the risen Lord still powerfully alive is the "real Jesus." On the other side, Jesus must be understood apart from the framework of the Christian creed: the resurrection is reduced to a series of visionary experiences of certain followers, and the significance of Jesus is to be assessed entirely from the period of his ministry.

Different perceptions of the Christian religion are also operative. One perspective views Christianity as based in God's self-disclosure or revelation, and therefore structured and enlivened by that self-disclosure. In this view, Christianity is regarded as a way of life rooted in and organized around a genuine experience of ultimate reality mediated by the crucified and raised Messiah, Jesus. The other perspective sees Christianity as another among the world's religions, that is, fundamentally as a cultural reality rooted in the human construction of symbolic worlds.

The same difference in perspective affects understandings of the Church. One views the Church as a community answerable primarily to the sources of its own identity, whose integrity is measured by fidelity to its originating experiences and canonical writings, whose teachers and teaching are evaluated essentially in terms of their commitment to and clear expression of those resources. Another views the Church as a social organization answerable to the criteria of the society in which it finds itself; its integrity is to be measured according to the norms applied to other social and political entities, in terms of its relevance or usefulness for the contemporary understanding and valuation of the world.

A final contrast concerns the New Testament and, in particular, the Gospels. From one side, the New Testament is regarded as a collection of texts that, if not divinely inspired, are at least authoritative and revelatory, giving access to the truth about Christianity's deepest convictions and experiences. The Gospels are perceived as reliable scripts for a true apprehension of "the real Jesus" consonant with the Church's continuing experience of him as risen Lord. From the other side, the New Testament is seen primarily as a collection of ancient writings whose main value is to provide historical information concerning the origin and development of the Christian religion. From this point of view, the "faith perspective" of the texts themselves must be countered by a critical and sometimes skeptical reading of the sort generated by a "hermeneutics of suspicion." The Gospels represent the prime example of the problem presented by the faith perspective; they are narratives requiring deconstruction in order for the "real Jesus," that is, the "historical Jesus," to be seen.

Each set of perceptions has its own internal logic. The first could appropriately be called that of "faith," understood as the complex of Christian convictions and self-understandings. The other set might justly be termed that of "historical criticism," understood as the complex of intellectual convictions based not on the authority of revelation and issuing in theology but on the authority of human intelligence and issuing in the human sciences, including the study of religion.

In a tidy world, each set of perceptions would have a single social location. The perceptions of faith would belong in a Church that was dedicated entirely to the articulation of faith in distinctive patterns of life, and that read the New Testament as the paradigmatic expression of that faith and those patterns. The perceptions of historical criticism would be located in an academy dedicated entirely to the free play of scholarship and to the critical investigation of all received traditions.

In fact, however, the connection between ideologies and social structures is today not nearly so neat. Instead, there are complex and constantly changing boundaries between a variety of versions of the church and a variety of realizations of the academy. Some understanding of this shifting and unstable situation is required if we are to understand the harshness of the contemporary Historical Jesus debate, as well as its confused and largely unfocused character. The dissemination of the debate through the media reveals the disheveled, distraught, and depressed condition of both Church and academy as American culture slouches toward the millennium.

A Culturally Divided Church

Despite the ecumenical movement—which has largely concerned itself with matters of doctrine and ritual—Christianity in America is today profoundly divided. The lines of division are not, however, primarily the traditional ones by which heresy and orthodoxy were determined. Christians today are divided by their commitments to certain cultural perceptions. The division can be stated simply as a contrast between the attitude that welcomes and affirms that view of the world deriving from the time of the Enlightenment, which is usually called modernity, and the attitude that explicitly rejects that worldview.

Modernity as a worldview can be stated in terms of the ancient debate between Protagoras and Plato. Protagoras insisted that "man" was the measure of all things. Plato countered that God is the measure of reality. A primary reason why early Christians regarded Plato as the best of philosophers was precisely this respect for the divine as absolute, and his view was taken as axiomatic for the long centuries of Christendom. The Enlightenment represented a return to Protagoras. Reality is not measured by the divine mind expressed in revealed texts, but by the human mind expressed in scientific inquiry.

The distance between the two starting points is enormous and perhaps unbridgeable. When faced with the question of whether wine passed through the lungs before entering the stomach, the philosopher Plutarch argued from authority: the differing opinions of earlier thinkers were assessed in terms of their overall authority as teachers. Confronted with the same question, Francis Bacon would say: open a cadaver and let's examine human anatomy.

For those who embraced it, the Enlightenment represented liberation from the shackles of dogma, superstition, and priestcraft (all considered more or less equivalent). The essential tool of the Enlightenment project was critical history. Beginning with Lorenzo Valla's demonstration that the Donation of Constantine (supposedly a legal document deeding rule over Europe to the pope) was a forgery, critical history progressed steadily against other claims of the church. It did not take long for historians to challenge the sacred stories of the Bible and lay them bare to the eyes of critical scrutiny.

Bit by bit, the medieval assumption that "the real world" and "the biblical world" were more or less coextensive came under assault. World exploration and the discovery of ancient and diverse cultures made it impossible to subsume, as Augustine's *City of God* had done, world history within biblical chronology and geography. Criticism convincingly challenged the traditional dating and authorship of books. Finally, the veracity of the stories themselves came into question. When the creation accounts, the Exodus, and the Exile were in turn challenged for their historicity, Christians sometimes practiced strategic defeat: this or that aspect of the Bible could be relegated to myth or legend, but the "important stuff" remained true.

What was seldom noted, however, was that both attackers and defenders had accepted the same definition of truth. The greatest triumph of the Enlightenment was to convince all parties that empirically verifiable truth, in this case historical truth, was the only sort of truth worth considering. Historical truth, furthermore, was measured in terms of referentiality: did the biblical account match something in the extratextual world?

It was inevitable that "the important stuff" itself would come under siege, and that historical criticism, in the name of intellectual integrity, would turn to Jesus and Christian origins. The entire first "Quest of the Historical Jesus" was in effect the battle over historical truth being carried to the neighborhoods where Christians wanted to live. Was Jesus "really" who the creeds of the church declared him to be? How could this be determined? By historical inquiry, of course!

The diverse responses of Christians to the challenge posed by modernity can (too simply) be placed within four basic patterns: active/accommodating, passive/accommodating, active/resistant, and passive/resistant. The easiest options to describe are the two extreme poles. The passive/resistant simply proceeds as though the Enlightenment had never happened. This response broadly characterizes Orthodox Christianity, whose "Holy Tradition" has functioned as a prophylaxis against a genuine encounter with the Enlightenment challenge. The active/accommodating response, in turn, is perhaps best represented by Universalist Unitarianism: the framework of modernity is taken as normative, and Christianity must fit itself as best it can into that framework.

The active/resistant response is the most obvious and visible. It regards the challenge of modernity (and therefore of historical critical inquiry) as a threat not only to specific biblical passages or particular tenets, but to the entire perception of the world given by faith. Before the Second Vatican Council, this response was most forcefully represented by Roman Catholicism. Today, the broad spectrum of conservative Protestant groups that are variously termed evangelical, fundamentalist, pentecostal, and millenarian most clearly represent this position.

The passive/accommodating response is the most ambiguous. On the one hand, it accepts modernity as something that not only will not disappear but must be dealt with for Christianity truly to exist in the contemporary world. On the other hand, this position has no clear and consistent norm for distinguishing between what is positive and beneficent in modernity and what is dangerous and reductive. It seeks to hold on to the traditions of faith even as it embraces a world that finds them unintelligible. This response has been found primarily in what are sometimes called mainline Protestant traditions, and after the Second Vatican Council, in Roman Catholicism as well.

Christian communities can be distinguished from one another, therefore, by their responses to modernity. Equally important, Christian communities are divided from within—often fiercely—on the same basis. The recent battles within American Lutheranism, Roman Catholicism, and the Southern Baptist Convention have all centered fundamentally on the question of the particular communion's response to modernity. It should be no surprise that key battlegrounds for such clashes are denominational seminaries. Adherence to the correct "cultural creed" (whether conservative or liberal) is increasingly a litmus test for faculty within seminaries and divinity schools.

The conservative administrators seeking to purge "liberals" from seminary faculties are not necessarily pigheaded and anti-intellectual. However inarticulately and clumsily, they recognize that the shaping of future ministers' minds is of critical importance for the future identity of a denomination, and that the shaping of those minds within the framework of modernity (again, symbolized by "historical criticism") is not neutral. It may have fundamental importance for the ability of an alternative construal of the world to survive. Indeed, it might be argued that the Jerry Falwells and Cardinal Ratzingers of this age have a sharper intellectual grasp of the cultural consequences of such seminary training than do their liberal counterparts who appeal simply to the ideal of academic freedom.

The active/resistant option would like to think that it is defending tradition against the corrosive acids of rationalism. But in its fundamentalist version, the conservative stance is profoundly paradoxical, for it seeks to root Christian convictions precisely in the *historicity* of the biblical accounts. By so doing, it finds itself co-opted by the very framework of modernity it is sworn to oppose, for it accepts the crudest form of the correspondence theory of truth as its own, and it enters into the debate seeking to ground the truth of the Gospels in their referentiality.

Conservative Christians also perceive themselves as culturally and intellectually marginalized. Their opponents are not only "liberal" politicians and "the liberal media," which they with some justice perceive as hostile to their convictions, but also "liberal Christians," whom they regard as fifth columnists, claiming to be Christian but eroding the faith from within. The conservative Christian response to marginalization has in recent years been aggressive. The most obvious sign of its active engagement in the "culture war" is its overt political agenda. The attempt to "reclaim" the cultural heritage of America as Christian lies behind the explicit support given to conservative politicians. The desire to overturn legislation concerning sexual morality, abortion, and prayer in the schools is connected to the deep sense that the only way the true Christian identity can be secure is within a culture that reinforces rather than despises it.

The same aggressive cultural agenda lies behind the conservative Christian entry into mass media, in particular through what has come to be called televangelism. The tactical brilliance of this technological end-run is obvious. The "liberal bias" of the media that despises the cultural backwardness of the fundamentalists can be bypassed and neutralized by the purchase of a satellite, which enables the broadcast of the true gospel (and all its cultural correlatives) directly to the people. At the same time, local churches perhaps less reliable in their preaching can also be circumvented, and the latent longing for "real religion" among the disaffected in mainline denominations can be tapped.

The actual use of the Bible in conservative groups, however, is sometimes puzzling. Anyone who has spent many hours (as I have) in fascination at televangelists' practicing their unique combination of religion and marketing knows that such preachers actually do very little real interpretation of Scripture. In this context, the Bible is less a text to be read than a talisman to be invoked. The fundamentalists' claim to take the literal meaning of the New Testament seriously is controverted by their neglect of any careful or sustained reading.

What they take seriously are claims about the *authority* of the Scripture: its divine inspiration, its inerrancy, its holiness. But as a source of meaning, the text is rarely engaged. When texts are used at all, they are lifted atomistically from their context as adornment for a sermon or lesson that has not in any fashion actually derived from the text. Such a method (if it can be called such) of using the New Testament enables fundamentalists to make claims about inerrancy and noncontradiction in the Gospels, because they have never actually engaged the texts in a way that would enable some basic critical issues to emerge.

A more complex pattern of avoidance can be found among those professors of New Testament in conservative seminaries who have managed to combine "critical scholarship" with the demands of traditional authority. A careful reading of their publications reveals that the scholarship is "critical" in form much more than in substance; the paraphernalia of the academy are used—often with considerable cleverness—to support conclusions already determined by doctrine.

The response to modernity by liberal Christians has been more positive, and the embrace of historical critical approaches to the Bible more emphatic. Within such groups, however, there has been a correspondingly diminished affirmation of the canon and the creed. Although the passive/accommodating stance tries to maintain a tension by continuing to assert tradition, the acceptance of modernity's categories as the ones requiring engagement automatically relaxes the tension considerably.

The result has been paradoxical, although perhaps predictable. The churches representing this stance (mainline Protestants and post–Vatican II Catholics) do not see themselves marginalized culturally or intellectually, but they do find themselves in decline. To the degree that this form of Christianity has assimilated itself to the dominant ethos, reasons for anyone joining it are harder to come by. We see, then, a fascinating phenomenon: the form of Christianity most explicitly at odds with modernity is enjoying the greatest success in terms of growth and real political influence, while the form of Christianity that seeks to accommodate itself to modernity verges ever closer to the margins of irrelevancy and even extinction.

Even mainline Christian groups, however, find themselves divided along cultural fault lines that are defined, once more, in seminary education. For generations, the clergy of these denominations have been prepared for ministry in seminaries or schools of theology where the categories of modernity have shaped scholarship, and above all biblical scholarship. First-year students, who often come to seminary with deeply conservative convictions concerning the inspiration and inerrancy of the Scripture, are exposed at once to the "shock therapy" of the historical critical method. They are told by eminent professors, often in tones of scarcely contained glee, that everything they ever believed is wrong, and that to be part of this new academic environment they must accept the "historical critical view" of the Bible.

Responses vary. Some students find the attack on their convictions concerning the Bible just the sort of "assault on their faith" they had been warned to expect from liberal seminaries. They adapt just enough to get by, but upon graduation return to the uncritical views they had originally held. Their advantage is that they can at least continue to speak the language of their people. Other students "convert" to the new authority structure of the historical critical method. They learn how to dissect the Gospels into sources, correlate Pauline letters to ancient disputes, trace the development of Christianity from charismatic movement to church. They are socialized into a world that is dominated by history as the measure of truth. When they find that the Gospels dissolve under criticism, and that very little can be said about "the historical Jesus," they feel themselves left with little useful from the exercise. Having learned a new lore, they find that it serves no purpose for their work as ministers. They are incapable, in a sermon, of simply declaring, "Jesus said," without a ten-minute excursus on the problem of the historical Jesus. A little knowledge proves to be not only dangerous but actually disabling. Graduates of liberal seminaries who were successfully socialized into the academic world find themselves alienated from the world of belief from which they came and to which they are expected to return.

The popularity of liberation theology in many liberal Protestant and Catholic seminaries has only widened the gap between the critically educated clergy and the people they were called to serve. Such liberation has tended to base itself squarely on a "historical Jesus" that has been critically reconstructed from the Gospels after they have been subjected to the appropriate ideological criticism. The distinction between "Jesus" and "Christianity" is ideologically exploited. In the feminist reading, the "woman-defined Jesus" who preaches a version of female wisdom and displays all the appropriate gender-inclusive attitudes is supplanted by the patriarchal Paul, who, despite his nod to egalitarianism, suppresses women in his churches, and through his letters also suppresses women through the entire history of the church. In the Latin American reading, the Jesus who proclaimed a Jubilee year for the poor and followed an itinerant lifestyle is supplanted by the bourgeois tendencies of Pauline Christianity, which softens the countercultural edge of the Jesus movement. In the radical gay liberationist reading, the antiestablishment Jesus is declared "as queer as you or me" and the heroic enemy of heterosexist hegemony. Once more, Paul's statements against homosexuality represent the enemy. In each version, Jesus is pitted against the church, and the Gospels are pitted against the rest of the New Testament, but only when read against their plain sense to yield a portrait of Jesus that fits the ideological commitments of the readers.

Is it any wonder that ministers shaped according to such perceptions should find themselves with little sense of how the New Testament might speak to their own situation or that of their people? Christianity is reduced to a critique of patriarchal, capitalist, homophobic society. Sin is located in the structures of society, rather than in the hearts of people. In this understanding, talk about personal transformation, much less personal salvation, appears as counterrevolutionary. But these perceptions are scarcely those of the majority of Christians whom these ministers serve. Such Christians still expect a proclamation of the word of God that somehow is grounded in the gospel and pertains to the ultimate realities of their own lives, and not exclusively to the problems of the socially marginalized.

It has been precisely among the disaffected members of such mainline Protestant denominations that evangelical preachers have found their new adherents, among people who were raised within one form of Christianity but no longer find it proclaimed in their own churches. The most direct and devastating impact on traditional mainline communions has been made by the televangelists, who have bypassed the "liberal" academy and the liberally educated clergy as well as the liberal media in their "Christian" version of electronic direct marketing.

The same social configuration also raises questions about the precise intentions of the Jesus Seminar. In its rhetoric, the Seminar attacks fundamentalists and televangelists and claims that it wants to make the "real" Jesus available to people. But the only audience likely to be receptive to its version is the one already shaped by the presuppositions of historical criticism, namely, liberal Christians and liberally educated ministers. The Jesus Seminar, too, is preaching to the already converted. This makes its bypassing of the church all the more interesting. It matches the media appropriation by the conservatives with a media manipulation of its own.

The most serious question facing the various Christian churches in America today is connected precisely to their response to modernity. Is it possible for Christians within the churches to maintain allegiance to tradition, yet appropriate it and transmit it "critically," that is, tested by intelligent inquiry? Or must the options be the sort that divide Christians into mutually antagonistic and noncommunicating camps? Are the only options a simplistic assertion of Scripture's inspiration, authority, and inerrancy, accompanied by a refusal to take the actual texts of Scripture seriously, or an uncritical adherence to "criticism" that in the name of intellectual integrity and freedom expresses contempt for the very qualities of Scripture most important to believers, namely, their ability to transform consciousness according to "the mind of Christ"? So long as "critical inquiry" is identified with "historical criticism," those may be the only options available, and the present divisions are likely to grow even deeper. We will need to ask in subsequent chapters, however, whether that equation is a necessary one.

A Confused State of Scholarship

In a simple version of culture war, hostile criticism would be pitted against belief, and each position would be located in the appropriate social settings. Criticism would find its home in the academy, and belief in the Church. But the reality is that the social locations of biblical scholarship are diverse, and the question of its precise purpose very much an open one. To properly locate the present situation, a rapid review of the development of critical scholarship within and outside the Church may be helpful.

Before the Protestant Reformation in the sixteenth century, biblical scholarship was carried out exclusively in service of the Christian faith, within the framework of the canon (the official collection of biblical writings), the teaching authority of the church, and the creed. Much of patristic and monastic interpretation, in fact, took the form of homilies to be delivered at worship. Even when the medieval universities developed out of monastic schools as independent centers of learning, biblical scholarship was done within the framework of theology, the "queen of the sciences," and the threefold norm of church, canon, and creed held sway.

The Reformation, especially through the work of Martin Luther, changed everything. Luther opposed Catholicism's emphasis on tradition as norm for Scripture by elevating Scripture to the exclusive font of revelation (*sola scriptura*). This made the key to right living dependent on the right reading of Scripture. The context of ecclesial interpretation was weakened further by the principle of individual interpretation, for the first time made practical by translations from the original, and above all by the invention of printing, which made Bibles readily available to the laity. Now the New Testament is not heard mainly in Latin within the liturgy and as expounded by clergy, but can be apprehended directly in one's native language and is open to private interpretation. It was a combination filled with potential conflict. Everything essential rested on the reading of a text, but that reading could be carried out by individuals!

Luther was from beginning to end not only an interpreter of the Bible but a passionate lover of the texts and of the One to whom they pointed. Nevertheless, his approach to the New Testament (which was to prove overwhelmingly influential in the development of critical scholarship) was deeply if unconsciously affected by the intellectual climate of the Renaissance. This can be seen not only in his preference for the recovered Greek text over the Latin Vulgate proclaimed in the church (note here the implicit authority of the Greek-reading scholar over the Latin-dependent clergy), but above all in his commitment to a certain kind of historical understanding. The recovery of the original text was the key to the recovery of original Christianity. Just as Renaissance scholars, once classical texts were recovered, could measure the inadequacy of late-medieval society against the grandeur of Greece and Rome, so could the theologian measure the inadequacy of medieval Christianity against the norm of the primitive church, or even better, the figure of Jesus himself.

Two important assumptions remain implicit in this commitment. The first is that the recovery of origins means the recovery of essence: the first realization of Christianity is naturally the best. It follows from this premise that any "development" of Christianity must be seen as a decline. The second assumption is that history can act as a theological norm for the reform of the church: the recovery of "original Christianity" made available through the recovery of the "original Scripture" should naturally serve as measure and critique for all subsequent forms of Christianity.

So widely are precisely these assumptions held—and taken for granted—that it is perhaps necessary to pause in order to assert that they are, in fact, assumptions rather than necessary truths. Only a little thought is required to realize the problematic character of the first premise. Indeed, in most matters, we now assume that earlier forms are perfected by later development. Likewise, it is by no means our automatic instinct in other matters to measure the adequacy or integrity of present behavior against the norm of earlier behavior. Rather, we tend to measure adequacy and integrity in terms of other criteria.

Luther's principle of *sachkritik* ("content criticism") also bore within it-self a seed whose growth would shape later critical scholarship. He was will-ing to assign authority to New Testament writings, not on the basis of their acceptance by the church (their place within the traditional canon), but on the basis of their theological worth. This mainly had to do with their Christology (those writings that "show thee the Christ") and soteriology ("*sola fide*," that is, we are saved by faith alone).

Fascinatingly, Luther also tended to connect these theological norms to historical judgments, especially concerning authorship. If a writing was not "apostolic" in its authorship, not christologically centered, and not sound on righteousness, it simply did not have the same value as the writings that were. It should be no surprise that the Letter of James, which in Luther's view failed on all three counts, was relegated to a position apart from "the proper books." In Luther, the framework of church and canon is weakened. In their place is a fateful link between history and theology.

Luther could never, I think, have envisaged a form of biblical scholarship that would define itself over against faith. But he inadvertently caused the crack that would later widen to a chasm. The "historical critical" approach to the New Testament and Christian origins that developed among German scholars in the eighteenth and nineteenth centuries surely owed much to British Enlightenment critics, but in their peculiar use of history as a measure for theology, they were direct descendants of Luther. Protestant, and specifi-cally Lutheran, presuppositions pervade critical biblical scholarship.

Increasingly, however, Luther's fight on the side of faith against the church gets translated into a fight for intellectual freedom ("a higher faith") against the benighted dogmas of Christianity itself (represented by official teaching bodies). In this battle, the emblem of freedom becomes the historical critical method, which is increasingly put in service of an ever-more-radical challenge to the received traditions of the church. In the mid-nineteenth cen-tury, the Tübingen school's dramatic recasting of early Christian history as a theological conflict between Pauline and Judaizing factions subjected the documents of the New Testament themselves to "critical testing" in terms of this theory. Since Paul represented the pure position of gentile freedom, his thought must have been consistent, so that only those letters teaching his supposed doctrine could really be from him. The rest of the Pauline letters, indeed the rest of the New Testament, could then be distributed along the line of theoretical development from Pauline to Judaizing to Catholicizing, according to the way their contents fit the assigned slot.

The version of early Christian history generated by the Tübingen school was so energetic, earnest, and at times brilliant that despite early, detailed, and meticulous rebuttals, its fundamental approach remains very much alive in the academy. Part of its continuing appeal is that it claimed all the virtues of the academy ("value-free" inquiry, freedom from censorship, scientific methods) while continuing the basic theological program of Luther (content-criticism of the canon, Pauline theology as first and best). Historical criticism, therefore, could perceive itself and be perceived as standing in opposition to received traditions and the church that propagates them. And this, despite the fact that most of this critical work continued to be carried out in the context of universities and seminaries that were supported by the church!

Such critical scholarship appeared even more radical and dangerous when applied to the figure of Jesus. Hermann Samuel Reimarus (1694–1768) regarded his writings on Jesus to be so inflammatory that he never published them in his lifetime. They were released by Lessing after his death as *Fragments of the Unknown of Wolfenbüttel*. No wonder: Reimarus denied the supernatural character of Jesus' ministry and interpreted it entirely in terms of nationalist hopes and political ambition. Reimarus argued that Christianity was based not in divine revelation but in human failure and fraud. David Strauss's *The Life of Jesus Critically Examined* (1835) embroiled its young author in a lifetime of controversy. No wonder: he argued that the evangelists created the image of Jesus as Jewish messiah out of a creative "mythmaking" process—finding in the Old Testament the symbols with which to clothe their narrative about one they were convinced had to have been the Messiah.

By no means did such radical theories sweep the field of New Testament scholarship. They were vigorously opposed by scholars who defended the veracity of the Christian claims. What went largely unnoticed, however, was that the *grounds* of the debate were entirely dictated by the challengers. Attackers and defenders of orthodoxy alike appealed to the evidence of *history* in support of their positions. The "historical critical method" was assumed to provide the only legitimate rules for debate. In the hands of conservatives, it yielded a picture of Christian development conformable to tradition. In the hands of liberals, it gave a history that called into question traditional positions. What had fundamentally eroded, however, was the framework of canon, creed, and church by which Christianity had defined itself in debate since the late second century. The creed was under attack, the canon was challenged, and the church's tradition was regarded as the problem.

For over a hundred years, the battle generated by historical critical scholarship continued within the context of the church and of an academy that was in greater or lesser degree supported by or responsible to the church. It would be a mistake to think that those who argued from the side of historical critical scholarship saw themselves as apostates from Christian faith. On the contrary, they perceived themselves as the more genuinely Christian for having broken free from the shackles of dogma and superstition. They took it as their mission within faculties of theology to "convert" their students to "higher criticism," which in their eyes meant also a higher and purified form of Christianity. But it was a form of Christianity that often had no institutional allegiance and equally often expressed contempt for the ideas and practices of actual Christian communities.

The "modernist/fundamentalist" controversy in the early years of the twentieth century gave a peculiarly American flavor to the tension created by the ideological split between liberal scholars and conservative pastors, and led increasingly to the desire on the side of scholars for a social location that owed nothing to the church. Within the great private universities of this country that had some historical connections to churches but over the years had increasingly taken on a secular character, departments of religious studies began to be developed not only for the purposes of undergraduate education within the humanities, but also as centers of graduate research.

The study of the New Testament and Christian origins within the context of the "study of religion," it was thought, would cut the centuries-old tension between church and academy cleanly. Scholars would now be answerable only to the criteria of scholarship rather than to church tradition. The study of religion could be carried out in the value-free and neutral environment of the other human sciences, having as its conversation partners not only (or even especially) theology, but disciplines such as philosophy, history, classics, linguistics, anthropology, psychology, and sociology.

In just such a context, it could be imagined, critical scholarship on the Bible could also perform a distinctively valuable social function. Undergraduates formed by primary socialization in the churches could have their traditional values examined and tested by the critical study of the Bible in the same way that their traditional social and political values were tested and examined by courses in economics and political science. Just as those courses did not disqualify young people from lives of economic and political activity, it could be argued, so would courses critically examining religion not disable them from involvement with the life of the church; the main difference would be that their engagement would be more mature and "critical."

Biblical scholarship in America increasingly found its home to be secular universities and schools of theology related to such universities (e.g., Chicago, Harvard, Yale), where the fundamental commitment was to the intellectual life, rather than denominational seminaries that were committed primarily to the formation of clergy for the church. The New Testament continued to be studied in both locales. But the intellectual center of gravity was undeniably in the universities. Then, precisely when the post–World War II expansion of the American university system was at its height, the Supreme Court opened the way for the establishment of religious studies programs in *state* universities. The sociological shift in biblical studies became even more visible. Suddenly there was a need to produce thousands of Ph.D.s in biblical studies to staff new undergraduate programs across the country. The chief producers were the major secular religious studies departments. The teachers of undergraduates, in other words, were themselves trained in contexts that had little allegiance to theology in any sense, certainly not to Christian tradition or the institutional church. Within a few more years, state universities were themselves gearing up graduate programs for the production of still more Ph.D.s.

The change in the nature of New Testament scholarship can be suggested by the growth and change in the main scholarly guild for such scholarship in America. The Society of Biblical Literature (SBL) began about the turn of the century and had a membership roughly coextensive with the biblical faculty of the great old schools of theology: Harvard, Yale, Princeton, Union. As late as the 1960s, the annual meeting could fit the membership in a single hall. Growth in the membership led to the development of a subsidiary organization called the National Association of Biblical Instructors (NABI), aimed mainly at those whose fate it was to teach in the hinterlands rather than be researchers in great graduate centers. But in the 1970s, NABI changed its name to the American Academy of Religion (AAR), a learned society embracing not only the teachers of Bible but the entire complex field of religious studies as it was developing in universities across the land. The Society of Biblical Literature and the American Academy of Religion began having joint meetings. The annual national meeting now involves up to eight thousand participants. Thousands of other scholars take part in dozens of regional meetings throughout the country, and the critical study of the Bible is being propagated in annual international meetings in Western Europe, Australia, and now Eastern Europe as well.

From some perspectives, biblical scholarship in America is booming. More Ph.D.s are produced, more dissertations are written, more books and articles are published than ever before. The gains achieved by such a vast workforce are obvious: new archaeological discoveries and decipherments; texts known and unknown from antiquity edited, translated, and analyzed; new methods of analysis borrowed from literature and the social sciences. The sheer volume of *product*, however, poses harder questions about process and purpose. More scholarship is written than can seriously be read or responsibly reviewed. Disturbing amounts of inferior work are produced. Although the actual database for biblical studies is relatively small, the volume of secondary literature produced over the last two thousand years—in geometric increase over the past thirty years—forces scholars into absurdly narrow specializations: dissertations are written on aspects of the hypothetical document Q, for example, or on a set of verses from the Gospel of John, with no reference to a larger world of meaning.

The long battle for free investigation of the New Testament and Christian origins has finally and decisively been won in the contemporary American university. Now the question must be raised concerning the point of the freedom. What is the purpose or pertinence of all this industry, all this production of scholarship? What are the boundaries of its discourse? Is there a conversation at all, and if so, does it matter? If it matters, to whom? Is it the case, as a senior scholar recently observed, that the implied audience for most of this scholarship seems to be other members of the guild (who already agree with its presuppositions) and tenure committees?

The great increase in academic production within the university context has been accompanied by a decline in attention to teaching. Partly this results from the internal institutional pressures of the academy, which has focused almost exclusively on publication as the measure for tenurability. The best publications, furthermore, are those that are most "scholarly," that is, written for refereed journals and bristling with footnotes. In this environment, it is an understandable survival mechanism for professors to privilege research over their teaching.

But another factor has complicated the teaching of the New Testament within universities and even seminaries. Professors who had been trained in the historical critical method found a growing gap between their own sense of what New Testament scholarship was about and the needs of their students. The classic paradigm of critical study had flourished in a scholarship that located itself against tradition: students brought up within the traditions of a church could be moved to a more critical (and "better") apprehension of Christianity by passage through the "historical critical method."

The paradigm required students who already had a thorough but "uncritical" knowledge of the Scripture. Increasingly, however, it has become obvious that the breakdown of tradition, especially in mainline Protestantism and Roman Catholicism, has produced several generations of students who have little grasp of their own faith tradition, and virtually no knowledge of the Bible at all. The pressing need of such students is to have the tradition transmitted in the first place, as prerequisite to critical reflection on it. Scholars whose methods have been developed only in an antagonistic relationship to tradition are ill-equipped to perform that task. Too often in recent years, teachers have simply given up on the students, blaming them for a lack of interest in "serious scholarship." Too often, university professors have shrugged off student apathy at their lucubrations with a variation of the failed coach's alibi: "I taught good but they learned bad." Such dismissal is a form of denial, of refusing to recognize that the issue goes deeper than one of student apathy, and involves the definition of what biblical scholarship is really about and what its purpose is. There is, therefore, a crisis in pedagogy concerning the New Testament in colleges and universities.

More and more, it is a crisis that extends to seminaries and schools of theology as well, particularly in those whose faculties have been recruited from the most prestigious (i.e., scholarly in the sense described) graduate programs. There seems to be less and less fit between the exotic "methodologies" and "criticisms" taught in graduate programs and the human and cultural needs of ministers within churches. A fresh Ph.D. whose entire approach to the New Testament is in terms of "ideological criticism" (i.e., discovering all the ways the texts are oppressive to underrepresented persons) quickly runs out of insight pertinent to those whose work with the text demands weekly preaching, the visitation of the sick, and the comfort of the grieving.

Alienated from students who come to the study of the New Testament seeking the bread of religious meaning but are given only the cold stone of historical criticism, alienated from the churches who see their scholarship as at best irrelevant and at worst positively inimical to Christian faith, many scholars experience dissonance between their self-perception as cultural critics and the culture's studied indifference toward their efforts. Eight thousand scholars of religion descend on a convention city. They hold hundreds of lectures and workshops and sessions. The event gets at most a page in a back section of the city's daily newspaper. Small wonder, then, that academics such as those in the Jesus Seminar long for media attention that can confirm their own sense of cultural significance.

The current debate concerning the historical Jesus takes place across lines of cultural institutions that have for much of their history been intertwined, and are now in considerable disarray and confusion. Just as the church must face hard questions concerning its response to modernity and its ways of mediating the tradition for succeeding generations, so does biblical scholarship within the academy face serious issues concerning its methods and purposes. The crisis has little to do with constraints imposed on scholars from the outside. It has much more to do with the emptiness of biblical scholarship apart from communities for whom these ancient texts have real-life significance, and the inadequacy of the historical critical method to meet the questions of significance posed by our culture today.

The future cultural significance of academics is not going to lie in their ability to seize the airwaves, as tempting as that option might be. Something more than fifteen minutes of influence is required. Academics must rediscover the truth that the finest expression of scholarship is in teaching. Scholars must again become effective educators both of the young and of their peers. The deep relevance of religious issues for life in the world cannot be communicated simply in academic journals intended for the consumption of tenure-review committees. But neither can it adequately be communicated in the sound bites made available through the press and "Larry King Live." Academics are in a position to exert enormous cultural influence exactly where they have always been privileged to exercise it, in the sacred precincts of the classroom.

When I begin a semester, I tell myself, "Think of what Jimmy Swaggart could do with one hundred young minds obligated to forty-five hours of lecture time this semester! Think of what Socrates would accomplish . . . or Jesus." These are the examples that academics should emulate, and the competition that academics must take seriously, if they are to exercise the cultural influence that legitimately belongs to honest learning effectively transmitted. They need seek no other forum than the one already generously placed at their disposal by society, the classroom. But in that space, they must develop skills and capacities of communication that too many have neglected or taken for granted. They must above all develop models for studying the New Testament that, while lacking nothing in critical acumen, do not flatten the rich possibilities of those texts to the thin and distorted "history" that has too often been made the representative of biblical scholarship.

A Media Manipulating and Manipulated

Little more needs to be added to what was said about the media as cultural institution in the first chapter, except to point out its own deeply ambiguous position as mediator of the cultural war being waged over the figure of Jesus. The communications media in this country is itself caught between the opposing pressures exerted on the one side by its ideal identity as "the press," enabling it to exercise the first-amendment rights to both inform the public and form its opinions, and on the other side by its commercial identity, in which it runs advertising, makes a profit, and seeks to influence legislation concerning giant corporations.

The tension has existed as long as the "free press" has also been a "commercial press," and goes back at least to the time of Benjamin Franklin. In the present-day economy, however, it is more severe, because of the way in which media/communications has become a subset of the new cultural institution known as the "entertainment industry." In a world of megacorporation takeovers and amalgamations, the ironies multiply: *Time Warner Corporation* owns *Little, Brown* as well as *Time-Life Books. Time* magazine's editors then review books that are published by those subsidiaries. *Time's* writers review movies made from books published by those subsidiaries and produced by *Warner Brothers Pictures,* movies that often in key scenes show named products in a favorable light, while these products are also advertised in *Time* magazine, which reviews the movies without any significant mention being made of the fact that all these are subsidiaries of *Time-Warner Communications,* which doubtless makes healthy contributions through Political Action Committees to politicians who will pass legislation concerning the media. It is difficult to say, in such a context, exactly what the "freedom of the press" might mean. It certainly does not mean "freedom from undue economic influence."

The coverage of religion in this country reveals the weirdness of the situation. Insofar as the media exercises its "ideal identity," it tends to treat religion gingerly and negatively. The working press, after all, continues to self-select its members according to the mold of such cultural despisers as Samuel Clemens and H. L. Mencken, for whom religion was of interest primarily for its unerring ability to cultivate charlatans and fleece the gullible. This, more than a conspiracy of "liberal bias" (connected to the Democrats), tends to make the coverage of religion an afterthought when it is thought of at all. It is simply not usually considered a serious part of reality the way politics and business are. Few members of the working press know much about religion, anyway. If they went to journalism school, they were not required to take a serious course in religious studies. Otherwise, they work with the mixture of their own upbringing and the prejudices of their city editor for perspective.

The media is therefore ripe for the sort of manipulation engineered by the Jesus Seminar and its attendant flood of publications. It was not prepared for religionists who understood the present capacity of the news media/entertainment industry to cover only three things really well (elections, personalities, scandal) and has been willing to offer a five-year miniseries involving all three. Working to deadline, chronically understaffed in the religion department, without much understanding of or interest in religion in the first place, and with a professional ethics that demands little more than getting the facts and getting them first, newspapers and local television news programs could hardly do anything else than publicize what the Jesus Seminar gave them.

As I pointed out in the first chapter, not all reporting on the Jesus Seminar was credulous. Articles appearing in the *New York Times* and the *Washington Post* gave fair voice to opposing views; coverage in *Time, Newsweek,* and *U.S. News & World Report* was at least evenhanded, if not critical of the work of the Seminar. But these nuances appeared deep in the stories. More important for the impact of the Seminar was the sheer volume of coverage and, as I have noted, the headlines that constantly stressed the negative results and their supposed implications for faith.

The same tendency is found in an even more recent media flurry, this time devoted to the claim by a German papyrologist that several lines in a Greek manuscript of the Gospel of Matthew could, on the basis of handwriting analysis, be dated about A.D. 70, some fifteen years earlier than the conventional dating of Matthew's Gospel. It is an interesting claim, but mainly to experts in paleography. How was it covered by *Time* (23 Jan. 1995)? The headline reads, "A Step Closer to Jesus?" and the subhead, "An expert claims hard evidence that Matthew's Gospel was written while eyewitnesses to Christ were alive." In other words, an obscure claim by an obscure scholar on an obscure point has been fed into the Historical Jesus debate, this time on the side of conservatives. As I said, a media manipulated and manipulating.

In quite another way, the communications media is manipulated by conservative Christians through the availability of satellite technology to anyone with sufficient funds. Televangelists can bypass the press and electronic news organizations entirely, just as they circumvent local churches and critical scholars, in their astonishingly successful version of direct-mail marketing.

Fundamentalist and pentecostal and millenarian versions of Christianity are broadcast around the world, generating, not only through pledges but through the sale of books and tapes as well, untold millions of tax-free dollars for exploiters of this happy opportunity.

The inadequacy of the electronic media to deal with serious issues in any way except through sound bites and personality profiles would not be so grievous except for the fact that the American public is notoriously addicted to television as its chief source of both entertainment and news—in the case of tabloid television, getting both in one package. This is a public that does not, apart from isolated pockets, read extensively or critically. It is therefore more susceptible than it should be to the spectacular rather than the substantive. Especially in that part of the public already cynical about most churches (because they are too liberal) and wary of academics (because they are too destructive), the reporting about the Jesus Seminar cannot but have confirmed the worst suspicions about both cultural institutions, and increased its reliance on direct-market purveyors as the true representatives of "old-time religion."

Conclusions

Although a consideration of the cultural institutions of church, academy, and media does not advance us substantially in our consideration of what might be meant by "the real Jesus," it does help show why the debate up to this point has had such an odd shape. In response to a challenge to traditional belief that takes the form of a historical claim concerning Jesus, the church does not rise up in a unified and outraged rejection. Why? Because the boundaries between church and academy, and the negotiations between faith and historical criticism, are so confused. Academicians are both within and against the church. Clergy are both believers and critics of belief. So complex are the combinations that any significant conversation is virtually impossible, particularly when the most serious discussants do not enter into direct engagement, but use the media as the arena for cultural arm wrestling.

Given all the confusion, the virtual unanimity on two points is all the more significant. The first is the way that "critical biblical scholarship" tends to be identified with "historical critical scholarship." That is, history is assumed to be the fundamental category and method within which critical inquiry into Scripture must be undertaken. The second is the way in which history is taken as a measure for theology, so that a historical determination is assumed to have implications for the Christian understanding of the "real" Jesus.

If the conversation is to move forward on more responsible grounds, these two assumptions are the ones most in need of critical examination. We must find a way of asking whether there can be a critical scholarship that is not "historical critical" in the way so often assumed. We must also ask whether there is in fact a necessary link between history and theology, or whether these are discrete modes of knowing. Only when "history" has been questioned more vigorously for its possibilities and limitations as a mode of human cognition can we begin to move toward a more responsible statement concerning the historical character of early Christianity and of Jesus.

CHAPTER 4

The Limitations of History

Perhaps the most problematic aspect of the spate of Historical Jesus books is their authors' assumption that "history" is unproblematic. They apparently think there is no need to define what is meant when the term *history* is used, since none of them bothers to do so. The confident contrast made, without any further explanation, between "faith" and "history" assumes a shared understanding of those terms.

In fact, however, the nature of history and of the historical is deeply problematical. It is not clear how aware the authors of these books are of the problems. What is clear is that they are trading on popular rather than critical understandings. In popular usage, the term *historical* is often opposed, for example, to the mythical, with the assumption being that one refers to "what really happened" and the other to "something that was made up." In popular usage, the historical can likewise be opposed to the fictional, with the same implied contrast between what is "real" and what is "made up." In short, casual usage bears within it the implication that "historical" equals "true" and "nonhistorical" equals "false." The Jesus Seminar exploits this popular distinction when it speaks of its historical deliberations delivering "the real Jesus" in contrast to the "Christ of faith," who is by implication somehow less than "real."

It is important to sort out some of these claims. A good start is to consider in a straightforward way what the business of history is, what its problems and possibilities are, and how these apply generally to the study of early Christianity. Then we shall be in a better position to think more clearly about "the historical Jesus."

The Character of Historical Knowing

Popular equations are enabled by imprecise concepts and unexamined terms. The term *history* manifestly cannot be used simply for "the past" or "what happened in the past," any more than *historical* can be used simply as a synonym for "what was real about the past." History is, rather, the product of human intelligence and imagination. It is one of the ways in which human beings negotiate their present experience and understanding with reference to group and individual memory.

In its essence, history is a mode of human knowing. It is an interpretive activity. The stuff with which history works is human events in time and space, various kinds of records of such experiences (often but not necessarily written, and functioning basically as aide-mémoire), and the effort to make sense of, or interpret, such experiences.

The intrinsic limitations to this form of knowing are, upon reflection, quickly evident. It is clear, first of all, that a great deal of what human beings consider "real" escapes historical knowledge. If history deals with human events in time and space (granting that time and space are meaningful and not simply themselves a priori categories of cognition), it misses a great deal. At the lower level, it misses things like fingernails and facial tics that partake of the human but never really surface as parts of "events." At the upper end, it misses a great deal of what is most properly human, things like alienation and forgiveness, compassion and despair, meaning and value, love and hope.

Only with considerable stretching can these "realities" be called "historical." Yet, we insist, they are real. They are not necessarily "events"; they do not necessarily surface for our inspection; they may not enter collective memory. Nevertheless, they are often the most defining elements of our humanity. But they are not the stuff of history. Historical knowing is like a sieve that catches big chunks but lets much fine stuff slip through.

Even when we look more closely at the material history deals with best, "human events in time and space," we begin to recognize how slippery such cognition is. What constitutes a "human event"? We may speak of the "birth of the United Nations" 1945 as something that is inarguably a "historical event." And we are right. But what constituted it as an event? Who participated? When did it start? When did it end? If we press such issues, we become aware that to "do history," we must artificially edit out "stop frames" in the cinematic flow of human experience, must draw lines of demarcation that enable us to focus, describe, define, and interpret. Yet, if we are honest, we also recognize that even in this simple editorial act, we are already engaging in interpretation. Our *selection* and *naming* of something as "event" is itself constitutive of the "event."

If so obvious and epochal an event as the founding of the United Nations turns out to be more elusive the closer we examine it, how much more is historical knowing limited when it comes to less public and prolonged events. As a teacher, for example, I may refer to one of my favorite lectures as a historical event: "The Historical Jesus Lecture of 1995." But what constituted such a lecture, after all? Was I the only significant character in the event, or were its hearers also constitutive of it? If they were, then did it matter whether they understood the lecture? We could ask further, when did that lecture begin? Was it when I started speaking, or had it begun when I first thought of the topic and outlined the talk? When did the lecture end? Or has it ended? Will the lecture be over before the last memory of the last hearer fades? For this "event," after all, was not about moving boundaries and rearranging national territory, but about moving minds in a certain direction and transforming internal terrain.

The same sort of ambiguity attends the second component of historical knowing, namely, the records of human events. Such records are inevitably selective. Not everything that happens is recorded, nor is everything that is recorded preserved. Not everything preserved is edited, translated, read, or understood. The documentary basis of our historical knowledge of some "great events" is astonishingly slender. Some events from antiquity are known only by a single sentence in a single work, preserved in a single manuscript. Records of human events are also selective because they represent only certain perspectives and interpretations. Even the most material historical data, such as inscriptions, inevitably result from *interpretations* by participants or observers of events. Historical knowing is limited to what this fragile skein of evidence allows.

The third component of history is most explicitly interpretive. It seeks to take the often sparse and accidental evidence of past human events and connect them in some meaningful pattern. The point or purpose of such a construal, however, has been a matter of debate from the birth of historiography. One position has held that the point of history is constructive: the memory of the past should serve as the source of positive and negative examples for the guidance of human behavior in the present. The other position has held that the proper function of history is critical: the analysis of specific evidence acts as a corrective to distorted memory and current claims made on the basis of such memory. Both positions give implicit recognition to the fact that historical knowing is not disinterested knowledge. The search of "the past" is very much generated by questions posed by the present, and by debates concerning the shape of the future. Both constructive and critical historians are concerned with claims made in the present on the basis of an understanding of the past. Even the most positivist of historians, who insists that his or her only concern is to "get the record straight," must sooner or later respond to the question, Why should the record be straight?, just as the person who spends the whole day "just keeping my room straight" should be confronted with the question of why a room should be kept straight at such expenditure of time and effort.

The ideal of self-conscious critical historians is that "criticism" should be applied not only to the records of the past (testing their perspective, bias, interest), but equally to the ideological commitments of the present, including those of the historian. Part of the complexity and difficulty of the best historical research lies in sorting through the maze of subjectivity and self-interest operative not only in the past but also in the present. The difficulty of carrying out such self-criticism in a consistent fashion, together with the difficulty of even locating, much less allocating, the pieces of evidence of past memory, makes the doing of authentic historiography a daunting business and the examples of its accomplishment all the more worthy of appreciation.

Epistemology—the critical analysis of cognition—can become an irritant when it demands attention. This is because human knowing seems to work best when the subject is something other than itself. Aesthetic knowledge is better at discerning the beautiful in great art than it is at defining the nature of beauty and how the mind grasps it. Moral knowledge is better at distinguishing good behavior from nasty than it is at defining the nature of the virtuous and how the mind recognizes it. In the same way, historical knowing works best when it is puttering around with evidence from the past, but becomes progressively fuzzier when asked about the nature of historical knowledge. Fair enough. Excessive epistemology becomes cognitive cannibalism. But a little bit of it is important as a hedge against easy assumptions and arrogant certainties in any branch of knowledge.

The best practitioners of critical historiography, therefore, are careful to make clear the character of their craft as a limited mode of knowledge, dependent on the frailties of the records of memory and the proclivities of self-interest. No serious historian, for example, would claim to render the "real" event or person, whether the event was Pearl Harbor or the person was Douglas MacArthur. The "real" event in all its complex particularity happened only once and cannot be recovered by any means. The serious historian recognizes that a "History of the Attack on Pearl Harbor" is a construction by the historian out of the available pieces.

If the historian is fortunate, there are many pieces, many forms of evidence and memory, so that the process of criticism can better sort out bias and the influences of subjective experience. If the historian is fortunate, there is rich information as well with which to contextualize a specific event, so that guesses concerning cause and effect might take on a higher level of probability. What is most important, however, is that the serious historian knows and acknowledges that historical knowledge deals only in degrees of probability, and never with certainty. The best historians candidly acknowledge their inability to penetrate the "reality" of the past, and confess that their craft involves in equal measure the attempt to verify the remaining evidence and the willingness to exercise creative guesswork to supply the most plausible or probable version that the evidence allows.

Because of the necessarily fragmentary character of all historical evidence, and because of the inevitable role of interpretive creativity on the part of the historian, serious practitioners of the craft are characterized by deep humility. They above all know how fragile their reconstructions are, how subject to revision, how susceptible to distortion when raised from the level of the probable to the certain.

It is the complete lack of such critical awareness that makes the recent production of Historical Jesus books so disturbing to serious practitioners of the historical craft. Each of the books we have examined claims certainty concerning the "real Jesus" that its particular key to the evidence has made available. Yet they continue to develop images of Jesus that are remarkably diverse if not mutually incompatible. Recent years have seen the presentation of Jesus as eschatological prophet, as violent revolutionary, as member of the Qumran sect, as proto-Pharisee, as gay magician, as charismatic renewer, as mystic teacher, as Cynic sage. The combination of inflated claims and conflicting results should alone alert serious historians to a fundamental problem.

The Jesus Seminar has especially played fast and loose with the several possible understandings of "history." On the one side, its members seek credibility by invoking the language of critical historiography: they claim to be scientific, to assess the data without bias, to be free from the constraints of ecclesiastical authority. They say they are engaging in value-free research, letting the chips fall where they may. But they make these claims without demonstrating the kind of careful practice that is characteristic of critical history. We have seen that their criteria are highly subjective, that they do not consistently apply them, and that their arguments are frequently circular.

On the other side, the Seminar also claims the privilege of constructive history to provide an alternative version of Jesus that the world (and above all the church) is supposed to take seriously. Thus, its members move easily from deciding that Jesus did not do X but did say Y, to the conclusion that therefore he must have *been* this sort of figure rather than that sort of figure. Then they leap—completely without warrant—to the conclusion that this has implications for Christian belief. But the move from the indicative (that's the way Jesus was) to the imperative (this is the way you must believe) is not legitimate, for the simple reason that history—even the best and most critical history—is not the necessary basis of religious faith. History—even the best and most critical history—is not even the necessary basis for social action or political strategy. The "lessons of history" are not only constructions of human interpretation but are also inevitably subject to human decision. This is the case even for the most secular subjects of history, as we can see from recent debates over how "the lessons of Munich" should guide our policy with regard to Bosnia. Or are they the "lessons of the Bay of Pigs" or "the lessons of Vietnam"? I will argue in the next chapter that the disjuncture between history and faith is even more profound and decisive in the case of Christianity. For now, however, we should stay a bit longer with the limitations of history, specifically as directed to early Christianity and the figure of Jesus.

The First Christians and the Limits of History

Compared with some other world religions, for example, Buddhism and Manichaeism, the origins of Christianity are relatively accessible to historical inquiry. The New Testament itself was certainly for the most part composed before the end of the first century C.E., that is, within seventy years of the death of Jesus. Paul's letters (and probably other epistolary literature such as James and Hebrews) provide firsthand evidence for the Christian movement in its first three decades. The Gospels were composed between approximately 70 and 90 but also contain materials that go back to the earliest period of the movement. Best of all, the Acts of the Apostles provides a narrative account of the movement's birth and first expansion from Jerusalem to Rome, written in all probability before the end of the first century.

Letters and narratives alike, furthermore, are anchored in the specific social realities of the Mediterranean world, suggesting in every line dimensions of Greco-Roman and Jewish culture confirmable by a wealth of other evidence, literary and archaeological. Compared with Buddhism, which has no biography of Siddhartha until some seven hundred years after his death, and compared with Manichaeism, whose very existence as a world religion must be stitched together from fragments scattered across continents and centuries, earliest Christianity appears to offer the possibility for serious historical inquiry. That's the good news.

The bad news for the historian of earliest Christianity takes three forms. The first is the fact that for the earliest period so little evidence has survived from outside observers concerning Christianity. There are a handful of authentic but very brief references to John the Baptist, Jesus, and James in the writings of the Jewish historian Josephus; but from the great ocean of Jewish literature, there are otherwise only fragmentary, coded, and oblique references to Jesus and his followers. From the Greco-Roman side we have the cryptic and not completely comprehending observations of the Roman historians Suetonius and Tacitus; the precious firsthand observation reported to the emperor Trajan by his governor in Bithynia, Pliny the Younger; and possible allusions by the philosopher Epictetus. Only in the late second century does the movement come under the closer and more critical scrutiny of observers such as Lucian of Samosata, the physician Galen, and the philosopher Celsus. The outsider information is of great value in establishing the existence and appearance of the movement as it emerged in Greco-Roman civilization, and it clearly helps to connect this religious movement with Jesus the Galilean. But the evidence is relatively so late and so fragmentary that it offers little by way of real controls for the much vaster evidence produced by the movement's adherents.

The second form of bad news for the historian is that this insider literature is precisely that: writings produced out of experiences and convictions concerning the ultimacy of Jesus as the revelation of God. The New Testament is, from beginning to end, religious literature. It is written by those who confess Jesus as Lord for others who also confess Jesus as Lord. The literature *as we now have it,* furthermore, understands by the designation "Lord" that Jesus, a Jewish man who was executed by crucifixion under the Roman procurator Pontius Pilate (facts, by the way, asserted also by Josephus and Tacitus), now lives in a more powerful fashion than in his human life, has become "life-giving Spirit," and continues to be experienced among his followers precisely through the transforming power of the Holy Spirit. This faith conviction generated the literature, permeates the literature, and cannot be expunged from the literature. For the religious reader, this faith perspective is not a problem but the point. For the historian, it means that a high degree of authorial bias must be taken into account when assessing the historical character of the New Testament compositions.

At this juncture, it may be helpful to pause and respond to the inevitable question: haven't all the archaeological discoveries of the past forty years opened up exciting new sources for the historical analysis of earliest Christianity? What about the Dead Sea Scrolls with their alleged connections to Jesus and John the Baptist, mined so extensively by Barbara Thiering? What about the Nag Hammadi library with its *Gospel of Thomas,* so beloved by Crossan and the Jesus Seminar? Is not the situation now fundamentally changed? Is it not the case that the canonical writings of the New Testament are no longer the exclusive or even the most important sources for the history of the Christian movement? The short answer, alas, is no. The situation has not fundamentally changed.

The discovery of the Dead Sea Scrolls in 1947 was revolutionary because it provided previously unavailable and precious insight into the varieties of Judaism in first-century Palestine, and into the workings of a sectarian Judaism making claims analogous to those made by the Christians. But the sober conclusion of the best-informed scholars (who are *not* members of a cabal seeking to keep the truth from the public) is that the Dead Sea Scrolls do not shed any direct light either on Jesus or on the development of Christianity. The very fact that Barbara Thiering has to work so hard against the obvious grain *both* of the New Testament and of the Qumran documents in order to make her case is itself evidence for the position opposite her own.

The same is true for the library discovered at Nag Hammadi in 1947. The diverse set of writings buried by Egyptian monks in the late fourth century provides exciting if puzzling evidence for the variety of manifestations of that form of Christianity that surfaced in the mid-second century and bore the designation "Gnosticism." But the compositions in the library, scholars agree, do not come from a period earlier than the mid-second century. Even those who argue that the *Gospel of Thomas* may contain very early Jesus material do not hold that the actual date of composition is as early as the Synoptics. Other scholars find more persuasive the position that the *Gospel of Thomas* presupposes knowledge and use of the canonical Gospels. Once more, then, these discoveries are of interest for the patristic period more than for the period of Christianity's birth and first expansion. Despite all the excitement and expectation, it turns out that the canonical writings of the New Testament remain our best historical witnesses to the earliest period of the Christian movement.

The third aspect of bad news for the historian is that the writings now found within the New Testament are, for the most part, impossible to locate precisely either geographically or chronologically. To repeat (for the point is pivotal): the New Testament compositions, which are the main source for any historical reconstruction, are themselves in need of historical location, which analysis alone cannot supply! The problems of New Testament chronology are multiple and complex, but the upshot is that although we can place Jesus' ministry between the years 28 and 33 with some confidence, trying to determine with more precision its exact beginning or ending is notoriously difficult. As for the earliest days of the Christian movement itself, the only hope for an absolute chronology is provided by the Acts of the Apostles. Because of the serendipitous coincidence of Paul's arrival and stay at Corinth (Acts 18:1–17) with two other events datable from extra-Christian sources (the expulsion of the Jews from Rome under Claudius and the proconsularship of Gallio in Corinth), there is the possibility of establishing a chronological sequence for the events reported by Acts. This chronology is, however, itself limited. It is of value primarily for placing a significant part of Paul's active ministry in the region of Achaea and Asia Minor between 49 and 57 C.E. But the movements of one missionary and his associates, no matter how important, scarcely amount to a portrayal of the movement as a whole.

The chronological controls provided by Acts (themselves established by means of analysis) are useful only for Paul and his associates, and then only in a limited fashion. They help us date and locate the place of composition (with some probability) of five of Paul's letters: 1 and 2 Thessalonians, 1 and 2 Corinthians, and Romans. Even for such important compositions as Paul's Letter to the Galatians, the question of date and place cannot be answered with certainty; it could have been written early in Paul's ministry, or later; it could have been written to churches in south Galatia or north Galatia. Only five of Paul's letters, then, can be placed with a fairly high degree of probability, and within an absolute chronology only with the aid of Acts. Without Acts, there could be no way of determining the sequence of these five letters. Even with Acts, the majority of the letters attributed to Paul (eight of thirteen) float free of any demonstrable chronological placement. And Paul is the historian's most certain point of reference!

The remaining New Testament compositions fall outside the partial Pauline chronology provided by Acts and a handful of letters. The dating of the four canonical Gospels is entirely a matter of scholarly deduction based on arguments concerning literary dependence and the possible window to historical circumstances provided by these narratives concerning Jesus. Suggestions about the geographical place of composition and the location of their readers are even more speculative. The conventional dating of Mark between 67 and 70, for example, rests entirely on solving the "synoptic problem" (the literary dependence among the Gospels of Matthew, Mark, and Luke) in favor of Markan priority, and then understanding the "apocalyptic discourse" of Mark 13 as a reflection of the tribulations experienced by Jerusalem in the war with Rome before the destruction of the Temple in 70 C.E.

Why are Matthew and Luke conventionally dated about 85 C.E.? Because they are considered to be literarily dependent on Mark, and some time must be allowed for Mark's circulation before revision by Matthew and Luke. These Gospels are also thought to provide a window on a stage of conflict between followers of Jesus and other Jews that would fit the late first century. Because John's Gospel is thought by most scholars not to be literarily dependent on the Synoptics as such, its dating is even more problematic.

The Gospels at least have as their subject a figure of the past, and provide information concerning the time of the evangelists only indirectly. An even greater problem is presented by writings that are occasional in nature but cannot be fitted within the Pauline chronology. There is simply no way to date Hebrews, James, 1 Peter, 2 Peter, Jude, 1 John, 2 John, 3 John, and Revelation with any certainty. The assignment of geographical location is also problematic for all these writings, although reasonable conjectures can be made concerning James and 1 Peter.

The problem is real and insoluble: the majority of the sources on which any historical reconstruction of early Christianity must be based are themselves impossible to locate historically because of the lack of firm geographical and chronological controls. History is more than chronology, of course, but it is deeply dependent on chronology. If the very sequence of events cannot be determined, questions of causality or even influence can scarcely be raised.

At the very least, such lack of external controls means that every attempt at historical analysis for the earliest period must involve some degree of circularity: the literary compositions are read as windows to the historical situation they address, and the reconstructed historical situation then provides the key to the meaning of the composition.

Leaping Limitations

The way biblical critics since the nineteenth century have sought so vigorously to overcome these intrinsic difficulties suggests something about the commitment of biblical scholarship to the historical method and something as well about the theological stakes the history of earliest Christianity was thought to have. As might be expected, historical criticism carried out in the absence of real controls could be turned in quite opposing directions.

Conservative New Testament scholars dealt with the problem by minimizing its impact. This was done first by giving maximum credit to the Acts of the Apostles as a historical source. In opposition to radical critics who considered Acts as an edifying legend governed by a theological agenda rather than historical facts, these scholars went to the opposite extreme, insisting that Acts was utterly reliable in every detail. Second, as much New Testament literature as possible was fitted into the Acts/Paul chronological framework. Thus, conservative scholars argued that all the canonical letters attributed to Paul were authentic, while letters like James and Hebrews were characteristically dated early. Third, traditions from antiquity concerning the origins of the New Testament writings (such as those found in Eusebius and Augustine) were given high value as controls over the literature. Such a strategy enabled the compositions credited to James, John, Jude, and Peter to be connected to traditions placing them in the apostolic period. Likewise, with regard to the Gospels, conservative scholars worked both to correlate ancient attributions of authorship to the character of the respective narratives and to minimize the critical problems posed by differences among the Gospels, by employing various harmonizing techniques.

Such scholarship—often massive in its scope—tended to confirm the picture given by the canonical writings. Historical inquiry served an apologetic purpose, namely, to secure the reliability and therefore the "truthfulness" not only of the texts but above all of the traditions concerning the texts. If this approach to the history of Christian origins lacked imagination or courage, it at least had the virtue of taking all the evidence of the canonical literature seriously. The controls that were available were respected, and the literature was read within those controls. The deficiencies of the approach were its failure to take seriously the diversity of early Christianity suggested even by the New Testament writings and its failure to recognize that the ancient traditions themselves were sometimes tendentious and in need of critical examination.

Other scholars took a far more radical approach to the analysis of Christian origins. With considerable variation, this is the approach that dominates scholarly study of the New Testament in the academy today. It begins by challenging the historical credibility of the Acts of the Apostles. Rather than a faithful account penned by a close follower of Paul either before or within a few years of his death, Acts is regarded as a highly tendentious theological writing of late composition whose account of Christian origins is from beginning to end legendary and edifying. Acts is taken to be the supreme source of the "myth of Christian origins" that is then extended and perpetuated by such orthodox historians as Eusebius of Caesarea. Since Acts, as we have seen, provides the only narrative framework for the first years of the Christian movement, its deconstruction is essential for any alternative version.

Once the framework of Acts is eliminated, then the pieces of the canon can be moved around in any number of ways. Nor is it now necessary to remain within the confines of the canon. Whereas conservatives appealed to orthodox tradition to throw light on the historical placement of the New Testament, the critical historians of the nineteenth-century Tübingen school appealed to the fourth-century pseudo-Clementine literature for clues to historical developments in the first century, just as contemporary scholars appeal to the Nag Hammadi writings.

But if the pieces are now all open to question, how can they be arranged in some sort of sequence? Since the time of the Tübingen school, critical scholars have been deeply dependent on some form of developmental model to provide controls on the data. For F. C. Baur and his colleagues, early Christian history was to be understood in terms of the conflict between ideas that worked themselves out inexorably according to the laws of Hegelian dialectic: the thesis of Pauline Christianity is opposed by the antithesis of Jewish Christianity, yielding as a synthesis early Catholicism. The beauty of this developmental model is that it enabled the pieces of literature to be distributed according to the "theological tendency" they revealed when subjected to appropriate analysis. And when arranged in the proper sequence, the compositions could then be read as though they were evidence for historical development.

The deficiencies of the Tübingen reconstruction were observed early and often: it treated history as though it consisted only in ideas; it saw development only in terms of conflict and opposition; it forced the data into predefined patterns; it was viciously circular in its method. The influence of the Tübingen school, however, has long outlasted its explicit rejection, because it provided the fundamental model for a historical reconstruction without the controls of the tradition or of Acts. It gave coherence and a sense of development to an otherwise unwieldy mass of evidence. For the Protestant scholars who employed it, the model was also theologically attractive, for it located the pristine ("correct") form of Christianity in Paul, just as Luther had declared. And since Paul was the first datable starting point, the movement from Paul to Catholicism had to be a movement from freedom to structure, from spirit to law. Development meant, simply, decline.

Other developmental models have followed in the wake. Many recent New Testament scholars use some version of a developmental model derived from the work of the sociologist Max Weber. This model has the advantage of focusing on social realities as well as ideas. But it ends up in much the same place. Religious movements (to render it simply) follow a predictable path leading from prophecy to priesthood; they begin as charismatic movements and end up as institutions in a process called the "routinization of charism." When this model is applied to the New Testament, Paul is taken as the starting point, now not as the teacher of "righteousness by faith," but as the prophetic figure who exercises charismatic authority. The remaining writings of the New Testament are lined up along a path leading to the institutionalized church. The end point is again early Catholicism: in place of charism and freedom and intense eschatology, there is static tradition, opposition to false teachers, reduced expectation of the end, and more elaborate organizational structures. In such a reading, the pastoral Letters stand at the end of a development toward institutionalization. And so on with other developmental models that have appeared.

What all such "histories of early Christianity" have in common is that they are not really "history" in any recognizable sense at all. The lack of real evidence is overcome by the heavy use of the principle of analogy, in the form of developmental models. The models provide the pattern and the meaning. The pieces simply serve as markers within it. The model uses only part of the data, and the data that is used is forced to fit the model.

Historians of early Christianity begin to appear like jigsaw puzzle solvers who are presented with twenty-seven pieces of a thousand-piece puzzle and find that only six or seven of the pieces even fit together. The reasonable thing to do would be to put those pieces together, make some guess about what *that* part of the puzzle might be about, and then modestly decline overspeculation about the pieces that don't fit. These solvers, in contrast, throw away the central piece, the Acts of the Apostles, that enables any connections to be made at all. Then they insist on bringing in pieces from *other* puzzles. Finally, they take this jumble of pieces, sketch an outline of what the history *ought* to look like (on the basis of some universal puzzle pattern), and proceed to reshape these pieces until they fit in that pattern.

New Forms of "History"

Two further developments in the past sixty years have made the pursuit of history in earliest Christianity even more problematic. The first is the widespread influence of Walter Bauer's 1934 monograph, *Orthodoxy and Heresy in Earliest Christianity* (English translation; Fortress, 1971). Bauer's study was a return of the Tübingen school with a vengeance. Like his nineteenth-century predecessors, Bauer understood the development of early Christianity in terms of conflict, and specifically conflict between opposing theological positions. But now the field of conflict is widened to include more than Tübingen's Pauline and Petrine factions. Bauer argues that the "myth of Christian origins" such as it is enunciated in the Acts of the Apostles—the myth that Christianity began in unity and only later suffered the ravages of disunity and heresy—is "mythic" both in the sense that it is untrue and in the sense that it provided a rationale for the victorious version of Christianity that sponsored Acts. The "true" or "historical" reality is that Christianity was first characterized by diversity, and only slowly and with some coercion by the Roman church achieved unity.

Much of Bauer's argument is brilliant. He was undoubtedly correct to recognize the amount of conflict reflected in the New Testament writings themselves as moving across a much more complex set of issues than those envisaged by the Tübingen school, and right as well to conclude that the question of what constituted "right belief" was not settled from the start.

There are also some serious problems in his analysis. Like his Tübingen predecessors, he reduces history to the history of ideas and envisages development entirely in terms of conflict. By using the terms *orthodoxy* and *heresy* anachronistically, furthermore, and arguing that in many cases the original form of Christianity was "heretical," he not only overstated what the evidence allows but also opened the door to include once more all the extracanonical writings (whatever their actual date of composition) as possible evidence for "trajectories" that might have gone back to the beginning. Once more, a certain imaginative construal of what "development" must have been (progression through conflict from variety to uniformity) enables the organization of the data, and the sense that "real history" is being done. Part of Walter Bauer's heritage has been positive for the doing of early Christian history. The recognition that earliest Christianity was characterized by variety is a healthy one. But part of his influence has been harmful, for too often the elements of unity in the earliest writings are slighted, and "diversity" is read in terms of contradictory or opposing movements rather than in terms of simple variety. As a result, the study of Paul's letters and the Gospels alike has been dominated for the past thirty years by the search for "opponents," and the attempt to restore or recover the voices of the opponents. The voices of those *opposed* by Paul and the Gospel writers, in other words, are assumed to represent other, possibly "legitimate" versions of Christian identity that the canonization of Paul and the Gospels suppressed.

This, then, is the second development: the recovering of the "suppressed voices" of earliest Christianity has become a boom industry, especially when the recovery of those voices can be used as leverage against the "dominant voice" of the New Testament writings themselves, which more and more are read in terms precisely of political struggle, oppression, and ideological warfare.

How can these voices be recovered? One way has already been indicated, namely, the inclusion of extracanonical texts. The discovery of the Nag Hammadi library gave tremendous impetus to this strategy. Here was a whole collection of "suppressed Christian voices." And since many of these Gnostic writings appeared at first sight to have a lot of positive things to say about women and a lot of negative things to say about authority structures, it did not take long for some scholars, like Elaine Pagels in *The Gnostic Gospels* (Random House, 1979), to argue that such texts should be read as the development of voices that the canonical writings had suppressed. Still others suggested that such texts should be included in a "reopened" canon. A closer look at the ways in which some Gnostic texts actually do speak about the female—for example, making cosmic woes dependent on the error of the female aeon Sophia, who must be rescued by the male Christ, and the *Gospel of Thomas*'s much-discussed admonition by Jesus, "Unless a woman becomes a man, she cannot enter the Kingdom of Heaven" (*Gospel of Thomas*, Saying 114)—muted some feminist enthusiasm. But the view of the canonical writings as suppressive of other "liberative" voices in early Christianity remains powerfully alive, and undergirds such influential books as Elizabeth Schüssler-Fiorenza's feminist reconstruction of Christian origins, *In Memory of Her* (Crossroad, 1983).

"History" now becomes a matter not simply of locating the voices within the canon, but of restoring lost voices to which—it is assumed—these canonical writings are responding. Behind every instruction of Paul there is assumed to be a contrary position enunciated by a rival or an opponent or a "suppressed group" within the Pauline communities. Finding Paul's opponents and identifying their voices thus becomes a major part of historical inquiry. But how can their voices be discovered if we have no writings from them? Obviously, their positions must be inferred from three sorts of evidence: (1) Paul's statements are taken as polemical/ideological, so each of his positions must have its counterpart held by an unidentified party; (2) such positions can be correlated with other information drawn from first-century Judaism and Greco-Roman culture; and (3) these voices can be placed in "trajectories" to other, later literature that gives more explicit expression to similar positions.

The classic expression of this method is Dieter Georgi's *The Opponents of Paul in 2 Corinthians: A Study of Religious Propaganda in Late Antiquity*

(English translation; Fortress, 1985). He reads every line in 2 Corinthians as a self-defense by Paul against his rivals, so that every positive affirmation or disclaimer by Paul can be taken by inference as evidence for positions held by his rivals. Since Paul preaches the cross and practices an apostolic style of lowliness, they must proclaim a glorious gospel accompanied by an apostolic style of wonder-working. This composite picture is filled out with data gathered from Hellenistic Jewish writings of the first century—Paul's opponents see themselves as "divine men" of the sort supposedly widespread in Greco-Roman culture and carried over into Hellenistic Judaism. This position is then placed within a trajectory—Paul's opponents anticipate the sort of early Catholicism and triumphalism found in second-century literature.

Georgi's work brought Bauer's premise of early Christian conflict into the pages of the New Testament itself. It was massively rebutted on key points in its argument. David Tiede showed that the "divine man" tradition in Greco-Roman culture was more complex than Georgi suggested (*Charismatic Figure as Miracle Worker,* Scholars Press, 1972). Carl Holladay demonstrated that the essential link Georgi posited in Hellenistic Judaism simply did not exist (*Theios Aner in Hellenistic Judaism,* Scholars Press, 1977). Nevertheless, Georgi's work proved vastly influential. His writing inspired a fresh examination of every Epistle, and even of every Gospel, for signs of the writer's "opponents."

Not surprisingly, many such "opponents" were discovered, so that even the Gospels could be read as responding to "opponents" or theological adversaries of the evangelists. The classic example is Theodore Weeden's *Mark: Traditions in Conflict* (Fortress Press, 1971), which argues that Mark's entire presentation of Jesus was in response to a "divine man" heresy held by Mark's opponents. The Gospel narrative therefore not only spoke about Jesus and the disciples; it also yielded a kind of "history" of theological conflict in "Mark's community" between a triumphalistic Christology and Mark's "servant Christology." Other Gospels have been read in the same way.

The genuine alchemist's stone of this new way of doing history, however, was the conviction that the literary compositions of the New Testament could, by subjection to analysis, be broken into discrete units that could then be regarded as "sources," not only for the composition in which they ultimately came to rest, but for the description of the period before they were incorporated. The remote antecedent for such analysis within biblical studies is the source analysis of the Pentateuch (the first five books of the Hebrew Bible). In that case, as popular books such as Richard Elliott Friedman's *Who Wrote the Bible?* and David Rosenberg and Harold Bloom's *The Book of J* have recently explained, various literary "seams" in the narrative (doublets, divergent vocabulary, disjointed sequence) were taken to indicate "sources" (J, E, D, P) that had been woven together (not altogether "seamlessly") to form the Pentateuch. On the basis of those *literary* observations, Old Testament source critics proceeded to make certain *historical* judgments concerning the dating of the sources and the situations that occasioned their composition. Thus, in addition to the "history of Israel" that was displayed in the narrative books of the Hebrew Bible, scholars were able to consider another level and kind of history revealed by the composition of the books themselves.

The method has been extended to every book of the Old and New Testaments. In the case of 2 Corinthians, the detection of "seams" has led to the hypothesis of as many as five "source" letters written by Paul, which were later stitched together by an editor to create our present document. The yield for this new form of "history" is obvious. Not only does 2 Corinthians now show Paul at battle with opponents, but it can reveal the *stages* of that conflict as well! If the "sources," which by now have become separate "letters," can be arranged in the *proper chronological sequence,* we actually have sources for separate moments in a conflict; we have, in a word, something that looks very much like real "history." The same approach has been taken to Paul's Letter to the Philippians. This short letter has been broken into four fragments. The fragments are then arranged in sequence to yield a "history" of Paul's deteriorating (or improving) relationship with the Philippian community. Once more, the analysis of a single writing appears to yield a complex "history."

But is it genuine history? Of course not. There is no new evidence, and there are no controls. All that has happened is that, on the basis of subjective literary judgments, compositions have been disjointed, anointed as sources, and then appointed to their respective roles in a hypothetical community drama. It is a paper chase, pure and simple. It is, indeed, like a house of cards. Pull out one element and the whole construction crumbles. If one "seam" turns out not to indicate a "source" but rather functions as a literary signal, then the whole picture changes. If the "sources" are shuffled in a different order, then a different sequence of events results. *There are no controls;* there is only imagination hitched to an obsessive need, somehow, anyhow, to do "history."

The same sort of analysis has been applied to the Gospels. The most obvious and disciplined way was through the development of "redaction criticism," which sought to find in the editorial changes made to their Markan source by Matthew and Luke some clues to the historical situation faced by the respective evangelists. Although subject to some abuse, redaction criticism at least has the control provided by Mark. Much more speculative (precisely because no real extant "source" serves as a control) are theories about the "sources" of the Fourth Gospel. And when Raymond Brown seeks on the basis of the Fourth Gospel and the Johannine letters to reconstruct the history of the *Community of the Beloved Disciple* (Paulist, 1979), speculation is subject to even fewer controls. Now the reconstruction of a "community," which is otherwise unlocatable either temporally or geographically, is traced through the analysis of four documents and the supposed stages of their composition. The problems inherent in such an attempt ought to be obvious. What guiding principles attend the discrimination between sources and stages? What reasons are there for arranging the pieces in the suggested sequence? What would happen if the order were changed? Once more, such exercises should be recognized as flights of fancy rather than sober historiography. I mention Raymond Brown as an example precisely because he is the embodiment of scholarly respectability and sobriety. His name is not associated with the fanciful or faddish. Yet his entire reconstruction of Johannine "history" rests upon no more solid basis than a series of subjective judgments and suspect methodological presuppositions.

James Robinson of Claremont and Helmut Koester of Harvard also spoke from within the heart of academic respectability in *Trajectories Through Early Christianity* (Fortress, 1971), where they explicitly embraced the Bauer framework, called for an end to canonical constraints when working on early Christian history, and in a series of studies began to trace "trajectories" of literary genres that, they argued, could yield insight into the history of diverse forms of Christianity. When Burton Mack, in turn, takes such "historical method" one step farther, the scholarly guild has very little solid ground on which to stand in criticizing his effort to read the "community of Q" out of a *hypothetical* "source" for the Gospels of Matthew and Luke. Nor can it much object to Mack's locating this hypothetical community in Galilee for convenience's sake, since a fair number of other New Testament writings had also been located there previously for no more substantial reasons. Indeed, the way toward Mack's reconstruction had already been well prepared by dozens of scholars and hundreds of books and articles that began with the assumption that Q was a real document and that it could, by means of literary analysis, be divided and subdivided into discrete "stages" of development. Mack may, in other words, represent a reductio ad absurdum, but the absurdum was already well represented in Gospel scholarship.

Methods and Madness

In this chapter, I have tried to trace the progression toward a certain kind of madness in the obsessive use of the historical critical method. Even though the subject of this discussion has been Christian origins rather than Jesus, I have considered it important to survey these recent developments because they throw light on the tendencies we have also observed in books devoted to "the historical Jesus." Here, as there, we find the same uncritical assumption of what is meant by "history," the same abandonment of a given narrative framework in favor of alternative explanatory theories, the same dissection of literary compositions into "sources," the same multiplication of hypotheses with no apparent controls.

Precisely the way virtually any hypothesis can sustain itself raises the most serious questions about the integrity of the biblical scholarship that passes itself off as critical history. At some point, the question must be asked whether an epistemological monism has not in fact distorted the very concept of history by insisting on discovering history where it cannot be found. Does the multiplication of contradictory hypotheses—each apparently with an infinite shelf life—suggest that this branch of scholarship really has no hard criteria at all with which to test theories?

Such questions in turn touch on the cultural crisis of the academy discussed in the preceding chapter. From the perspective of outsiders, biblical scholars are seen as pursuing lines of research that are not only deeply dubious but also profoundly useless. From the perspective of insiders, such chasing after shadows raises the question of the purpose and even meaningfulness of biblical scholarship.

Playing Within the Limits

The historical analysis of earliest Christianity is worth doing. But for it to qualify as genuinely critical scholarship, it must operate within the intrinsic limitations imposed by the scarcity of evidence and controls. A starting point is a more sober assessment of the Acts of the Apostles. Certainly the best recent work on this writing has demonstrated that it fits well within the conventions of ancient historiography, making an absolute distinction between "theology" and "history" distorting. It is possible, in other words, to recognize both the literary and religious intentionality of Luke-Acts *and* its fundamental reliability as a narrative framework for one part of the early Christian movement. But even as the necessity of Acts for any historical reconstruction is granted, its inadequacies must also be taken into account: Acts is selective in what it treats, and it creatively shapes what it considers. The evidence in Acts must be sifted very carefully indeed, and supplemented by information given by the other New Testament writings.

Even when all such information is taken into account, however, we must acknowledge that all we really have, beyond the outline of the movement's first expansion provided by Acts, is a series of sketches and vignettes of Christianity's earliest period. The Thessalonian and Corinthian correspondence does not give us the history of those churches, but a moment in their lives as viewed by their founder and teacher. The Letter to the Romans cannot provide us with the history of the Roman church, but one impression of it for one moment, in the eyes of a distant correspondent. We cannot even assert with certainty that the central place given Paul in the New Testament canon corresponds to his historical place in the first decades of the movement.

The non-Pauline literature that remains points to a fascinatingly diverse movement. But that literature also cannot be pushed beyond its capacity to speak clearly and without distortion. James the Brother of the Lord, for example, may well have written his letter from Jerusalem in the first decades of the movement, but his letter does not tell us anything about the history of the Jerusalem church, only the author's perception of typical situations among the "twelve tribes of the diaspora" to which he writes. The three letters attributed to John are less likely to give us the stages of a community conflict than a single three-letter packet of communication delivered at one moment in that conflict—a tiny window, precious to be sure, opened on a troubled messianic movement sometime in the first century.

The available evidence does support a substantial number of important *historical assertions* concerning early Christianity. It also enables us to assess with considerable confidence the *historical character* of the movement such as it appears in the records. And there are also some *historical events* in the first generation of Christianity that the most critical historian can affirm without hesitation. Can anyone doubt, for example, that beneath the sometimes confusing and conflicting accounts in Acts and Paul's Letter to the Galatians, solid evidence exists for a meeting between Paul and the Jerusalem leadership concerning the legitimacy of the gentile mission?

There are many other things that historians naturally desire to know that the sources can never disclose. Insufficient evidence exists to provide an adequate picture of the *historical development* of the movement as a whole in the first generations. More significantly, there is insufficient evidence to historically assess some of the *religious claims* made by the first Christians: claims to being possessed by extraordinary power; claims concerning visions and wonders; and above all, the most fundamental of all, the claim concerning the resurrection.

Reconstruction of historical development is not possible because there are not enough sources or controls. The religious claims cannot be assessed because such claims to transcendent experience are not available to historical assessment. Modesty is an important virtue for any historian and is particularly important for the historian of earliest Christianity.

With respect to the history of the New Testament period, then, the claim of "critical history" to have supplanted the internal myth of Christian origins is false. Not only has critical scholarship generated multiple and conflicting hypotheses, but these can be considered, in their own way, just as "mythic" as the one they seek to supplant. In the end, the "myth of Christian origins" turns out to have, in many respects, at least the same measure of historical plausibility as the theories that have been generated to replace it.

Finally, one of the most conspicuous failures of the historical critical method as applied to earliest Christianity is its inability to deal adequately with the compositions of the New Testament in their literary integrity. From the Tübingen school onward, criticism has involved the dismemberment of literary compositions. The purpose was to secure sources. The consequence, however, is that the New Testament writings—as writings—were neglected. While asking all kinds of questions of these documents that they could not answer, critics neglected to ask the kinds of questions they are capable of responding to generously.

The writings of the New Testament can respond to questions about the experiences and convictions that generated their composition, about the symbolic worlds used to interpret those experiences, and about the ways in which the interaction of experience and symbol created new worlds of meaning within the first-century world. Asking such questions of the text means probing their anthropological, literary, and religious dimensions. And in an odd way, these dimensions point to what is most interesting and most accessible *historically* in these compositions as well. The writings of the New Testament are not adequate to the task of reconstructing the history of the movement that produced them. But they are more than adequate to the task of defining the historical movement they in turn produced.

CHAPTER 5

What's Historical About Jesus?

Much of the excitement generated by the Jesus Seminar and recent Historical Jesus books rests on the claim that history can (and should) challenge Christian faith concerning Jesus. By peeling away the layers of uneven scholarship, media manipulation, and cultural confusion that make the present debate so lacking in substance, style, or satisfaction, I have tried to isolate this most central confusion concerning the nature and uses of historical knowledge.

In the last chapter, I identified some of the intrinsic limitations to history and applied them to the analysis of Christian origins. It is appropriate now to assess more directly the problems facing even the best-intentioned and most disciplined quest for the historical Jesus. What are the possibilities for genuine historical knowledge about Jesus? In what ways is such knowledge relevant or not to the religious claims of the classical Christian tradition?

Unavoidable Limitations

The art of history focused on an individual human person is called biography. As history seeks to do with the larger canvas of human events, namely, to order them in the proper sequence and understand them in terms of cause and effect, so does biography with the smaller portrait of a single person. The problems facing the enterprise are notorious even when the figure in question was on the public stage and there is copious documentation. The divergent interpretations of the life and presidency of John F. Kennedy, for example, demonstrate that the availability of virtually endless amounts of information does not guarantee unanimity in its interpretation.

In the ancient world the most obvious example apart from Jesus is Socrates. That he was a figure in the life of Athens toward the end of the fifth century B.C.E. cannot be doubted, at least in part because of the fact that Aristophanes, a contemporary playwright, attacked him explicitly in his comedy *The Clouds*. Socrates was also the hero in works produced by two of his students shortly after his death in 399. The historian Xenophon recalled Socrates' table talk in a work called *Symposium*, recounted Socrates' teachings in his *Memorabilia*, and gave a version of Socrates' defense before his judges in the *Apology*. Socrates also dominates the dialogues of Plato as the chief spokesperson for Plato's own philosophy. Plato's dialogues contain quite a different version of a *Symposium,* as well as a distinctive version of Socrates' *Apology.* The period preceding Socrates' court-ordered death also dominates the dialogues *Euthyphro, Crito,* and *Phaedo.*

It might seem, with such a wealth of evidence from both a contemporary outsider (Aristophanes) and insiders (Plato and Xenophon)—evidence, furthermore, filled with incidental detail about Socrates' adventures, relationships, and attitudes—that the "historical Socrates" would be fairly easy to reconstruct. In fact, however, the "real Socrates" proves to be elusive. Was he the charlatan portrayed by Aristophanes? Was he the sober, down-to-earth moral teacher recalled by Xenophon? Or was he the profound metaphysician who spoke through Plato's dialogues? The accounts cannot be altogether harmonized. Socrates may have been all these things, or some of them in combination, or none of them in the way reported. He was surely both more and, in at least some respects, less than any of the accounts about him. He was more in the sense that each account could only get at a facet of who he was or appeared to that observer to be. He was less in the sense that each observer brought something of himself into his account of Socrates, so that "the historical Socrates" cannot be distinguished, ultimately, from "the Socrates of his interpreters."

It was *this* Socrates, furthermore, especially the Socrates of Plato, that exercised "historical influence" on succeeding generations of Athenians and indeed on Western thinkers from Epictetus to Kierkegaard, and up to the present. Whether or not Socrates "really" fought at Marathon, or owed the debt of a cock, or was happily married, or was even the lover of boys, is less "historically real" than that he (through the memory of him in Plato) provided a fundamental example of a certain way of thinking and living and dying as a human being. Socrates' impact on his disciple Plato was undoubtedly so profound and pervasive that Plato himself could not distinguish between what Socrates "said" and he himself "heard." One could possibly disprove that Socrates said this thing or that; one could never disprove that Plato heard it in this way or that. The "remembered and interpreted Socrates," or, if one prefers, the "Socrates of faith," *is* ultimately the "historical Socrates."

The problems facing the seeker of the historical Jesus are even more se-vere. Although the biographies of Jesus (for the Gospels would surely be re-garded as such in the ancient world) were composed within forty to sixty years of Jesus' death, that is still later than the memoirs about Socrates com-posed by Xenophon and Plato. Socrates, furthermore, was remembered by disciples who were longtime companions and eyewitnesses. Although the Gospels undoubtedly bear within them evidence of firsthand sources and even eyewitnesses, such material is not identified as such, and the narratives as a whole were most probably composed by authors of the generation after that of Jesus' immediate followers. Finally, seekers after the historical Socrates have the benefit of Aristophanes' contemporary and highly critical observations to balance the "insider" accounts of the admiring disciples Xenophon and Plato. Outsider accounts concerning Jesus exist (as we shall see), but they are rela-tively late and are of uncertain value as a check to insider perceptions.

As for the Gospels themselves, the critical problems they pose the histo-rian are notorious. The most obvious and fundamental difficulty is that they are all written from the perspective of faith, a perspective that affects not just one part of the story or another, but the entire narrative from beginning to end. Despite sharing a faith perspective, the four Gospels dramatically dis-agree in their accounts. The greatest difference is between John and the three Synoptics (Matthew, Mark, and Luke).

All critical scholars agree that the reason for the strong similarity among the three Synoptics is that they are literarily interdependent. According to the majority scholarly opinion concerning this interdependence, Matthew and Luke both use Mark in the construction of their narratives, and each also uses separately a common body of tradition called Q, whether that designation refers to one written source or several. Each of the synoptic Gospels shades the story differently, but it is obvious that they tell the same story. The Markan "spine," which begins with the baptism of Jesus by John and continues through the burial of Jesus and the empty-tomb account, has been taken over by Matthew and Luke. The most pressing "historical" problem is whether this narrative spine is essentially accurate or whether it is entirely a literary cre-ation by Mark. In either case, the synoptic literary interdependence means that, for strictly *historical* purposes, these three Gospels in reality represent a single source. That is one of the reasons that some have been eager to spring Q loose as a separate source; it would then be independent of Mark and represent a second early source of traditions about Jesus.

In contrast, the Gospel of John does not follow the same narrative sequence as the Synoptics. In John, Jesus' ministry seems to last three years rather than the one year implied by the Synoptics. In John, Jesus works mainly in Judaea, in contrast to the Galilean concentration of the Synoptics. The differences in detail can be multiplied: in John, Jesus cleanses the Temple at the beginning of his ministry rather than at the end; in John, Jesus dies on the day of preparation for the Passover rather than on Passover day itself as in the Synoptics; in John, Jesus has followers at the cross with him, whereas in the Synoptics he is abandoned; in John, the empty-tomb story involves Peter and John rather than a group of women as in the Synoptics.

More significantly, Jesus does different things and speaks differently in the Fourth Gospel. In the Synoptics, Jesus' exorcisms are closely connected to the proclamation of the kingdom of God; in John, Jesus works no exorcisms. Instead, Jesus works seven "signs," as they are explicitly designated. In John's Gospel, Jesus speaks none of the parables that appear in the Synoptics and does not conclude short controversies with a pronouncement; instead, his controversies with opponents go on at considerable length and often lead to long revelatory discourses.

So many and fundamental are the discrepancies between John and the Synoptics that one of the earliest decisions made by the first "questers" for the historical Jesus was to abandon John as a historical source altogether. In hindsight, that decision appears precipitous. Further research has shown that elements of John's Gospel may well have value as historical evidence; equally significant, the confidence of earlier scholars in the bedrock solidity of the synoptic story line has yielded to the recognition of authorial creativity there as well. Settling such issues is not possible here, nor is it the point. The point I want to make is that the present shape of the canonical Gospels is not such as to encourage the historian.

It is not simply that the Gospels are divergent in their accounts. The historian must also contend with the fact that even if they agreed entirely, the Gospels could still yield only an extraordinarily limited amount of information. About Jesus' life before his encounter with John the Baptist, for example, virtually nothing can be stated with any degree of probability beyond the names of Jesus' parents, his hometown, and his birth in the time of King Herod. The reason for such historical agnosticism is simple. Only two of the Gospels contain infancy accounts, and they agree only on these points. The degree of variation on other matters—they have no stories in common, and have entirely different literary structures—makes agreement on these few points the more valuable. But the yield is not great. Only Luke reports the incident concerning the adolescent Jesus in Jerusalem. Even if it happened, and even if Luke's account were the soberest historical report, all we would learn from it "historically" is that the boy Jesus had a precocious sense of mission from God.

When it comes to Jesus' adult life, the Gospels give information for *at most* about three years. Contrast this with the years of Socrates' teaching in Athens! When the narratives are analyzed closely, furthermore, it is clear that they are relatively unconcerned with matters of temporal sequence, since the incidents recounted often appear in different order. Other editorial principles—topical, geographical, thematic—seem to have had at least as much influence in the arrangement of the narratives.

Not only the arrangement but also the selection of materials differs from one Gospel to another. To those who have not read the Gospels in this critical light, it is perhaps startling to realize that even Jesus' baptism is not reported as such by all four Gospels, and that some of the most renowned of Jesus' parables (the prodigal son, the good Samaritan, Lazarus and Dives, the sheep and the goats) are each attested by only one of the Gospels.

The very character of the materials chosen for inclusion by the evangelists, moreover, is dictated by considerations other than the purely biographical. They do not tell us anything about the "private" Jesus. By this I mean first that they are silent about his day-by-day routines and domestic arrangements. But more significantly, they do not reveal Jesus' inner thoughts, desires, doubts, and motivations, except as these are given "public" expression. The Gospels' selection of materials reflects a public *perception* of Jesus as teacher and wonder-worker, as charismatic gatherer of a following, as prophetic challenger of Israel, as suffering servant, as Messiah, as Savior.

Finally, the Gospel narratives contain stories that flatly confound histori-cal analysis. The synoptic transfiguration account, for example, is about a vi-sion experienced by three of Jesus' followers in his presence; in Luke, it is explicitly designated as an experience that took place during prayer. Now, even if this happened, even if it were "real" within the experience of those three persons, how can it be described as "historical"? Visions are not subject to confirmation or disconfirmation, for their only possible evidence must, by the nature of the case, be subjective testimony about a private experience.

The transfiguration happens only once. Stories about wonders worked by Jesus pervade the Gospel narratives. The easiest of these to handle from the perspective of the historian are the healings. But even here, we see immedi-ately that although it may theoretically be possible to verify that *something* happened (e.g., a person could not see and then after a certain point began to be able to see), or to disconfirm that something happened (e.g., the person in question could see all along but only pretended to be blind), there is no way to verify historically the essential claim of such stories, namely, that it was God's power mediated through Jesus that effected the healing. Such claims simply lie outside history's competence. The supreme example of such a claim, of course, is the resurrection, to which we will return later in the chapter.

In sum, the character of the Gospels as narratives of faith, the differences among them, the principles of arrangement within them, and the kinds of ma-terial they contain all make extraordinarily difficult the historical analysis *even of the three-year period* within which Jesus' public ministry occurred.

The accounts of Jesus' last days—called passion narratives—reported in all four Gospels offer a partial exception to these general observations. In con-trast to the episodic and loosely joined pericopes in the sections of the narra-tives dealing with Jesus' ministry, the passion accounts (starting with the Last Supper and extending through the burial) are remarkable for the way they pre-sent a lengthy, sequential, and connected story. Furthermore, they are notable for the attention they give to details, including the time and place that events occurred. Most remarkable is the relatively high degree of agreement among the four versions. Such agreement might be expected among the Synoptics, but in this case we find it also between the Synoptics and John. There is every reason to think that this part of the Jesus story reached some form of concrete and stable expression (whether oral or written) early on, and that its basic shape survived even the redactional work of the four evangelists.

The four passion accounts are notable as well for placing Jesus not simply among his followers along the byways of Galilee but at the center of great concerns in Jerusalem, before "rulers and kings." The story of Jesus, in other words, here intersects explicitly with the realm of "real history." Jesus is shown encountering well-known institutions (such as the Temple and the Sanhedrin), persons (namely Herod and Pontius Pilate), situations (such as the mob scene in Jerusalem at pilgrimage feasts), and historical evidence (such as that concerning the holding of trials, and who had rights to execute criminals for certain charges) about which we know more than a little from other sources.

In sum, the possibilities for confirming or disconfirming the *probability* of parts of the passion narratives being historical in character are much greater than for other parts of the Gospel narratives. But the exception is, I should add, only partial. In the passion narratives, also, we face the problems of differences among the accounts, discrepancies with outside sources (not all of which are so very much more "historical" anyway), and above all, the level of interpretation, which particularly in this part of the story (the place of greatest scandal, after all) is explicit and pervasive. Simply in illustration of the difficulties, I can mention in passing two books published recently. Raymond E. Brown's *The Death of the Messiah: From Gethsemane to the Grave. A Commentary on the Passion Narratives of the Gospels* (2 vols.; Doubleday, 1994), although devoted specifically to the interpretive aspect of each version, nevertheless is fundamentally positive toward at least the historical plausibility of much of the Gospels' accounts. In sharp contrast, John Dominic Crossan's *Who Killed Jesus?* (HarperSanFrancisco, 1995) argues vigorously against the historicity of key parts of the passion narratives, such as the trial of Jesus.

Historical Framework and Patterns

Sober consideration of such difficulties ought to reduce expectations of how much real historical knowledge can be gained about the year (or few years) of Jesus' ministry and the circumstances of his death. Complete historical skepticism, however, is equally unwarranted. A careful examination of all the evidence offered by outsider and insider sources justifies making certain statements about Jesus that have an impressively high level of probability.

Such statements do not concern details, specific incidents, or the sequence of events. They cannot get to questions of motivation or development. But they can speak to the most basic and important questions concerning the historical existence of Jesus and the movement deriving from him, as well as to some sense of his characteristic activity. It is precisely assertions of this order that provide the most important antidote to the less disciplined "reconstructions" I have surveyed. They also establish a framework of highly probable knowledge that other, more sophisticated and subtle reconstructions, like those of Borg and Crossan, need to take more fully into account if they are to win greater assent from other critical scholars.

The method used to establish this historical framework is one of locating converging lines of evidence. It is a simple method, based on the assumption that when witnesses disagree across a wide range of issues, their agreement on something tends to increase the probability of its having happened. When ten witnesses disagree vehemently on whether the noise they heard at midnight was a car backfire, a gunshot, or a firecracker, it becomes highly probable that a loud percussive sound occurred about that time.

Likewise in the case of Jesus, the convergence on one or two points by witnesses who disagree on everything else is all the more valuable. This is the case especially when the testimony comes either from outsiders or from insiders who are not creating but rather are alluding to narrative traditions. In the following pages, then, I will suggest some of these lines of convergence and the kinds of historical assertions about Jesus they allow.

OUTSIDER EVIDENCE CONCERNING JESUS

Good method dictates that we begin with outsider accounts. Although they are few in number, they are valuable above all because they do not regard the Christian movement as particularly impressive or unique. For the most part, outsiders regard Christianity to be a matter of superstition and stubbornness. Their slighting acknowledgment of the movement seeks to place it and its founder in categories generally recognizable to the culture. This is perfectly natural, for what constitutes an outsider perspective is that a phenomenon is regarded as "just another case" of something already known, just as the insider perspective is constituted above all by the insistence that this phenomenon is unique. The choice of categories used by outsiders, however, is important, for it can confirm or disconfirm some of the characterizations of the movement and of Jesus given by insider witnesses.

The biggest deficiency in the outsider accounts concerning Jesus is that, unlike Aristophanes' parody of Socrates, they are not the result of direct observation. The outsiders are either observing the movement that was associated with Jesus after his death, or relating what they have heard about the movement; what they say about *Jesus* in connection with that movement must therefore have been filtered through either other observers or the accounts of insiders as they were related to outsiders.

Three short references in Josephus's *Antiquities of the Jews* help at the very least to confirm the existence and chronological placement of characters in New Testament narratives. Josephus was a participant in and observer of the events leading to the disastrous war against Rome in 67–70 C.E., and wrote the *Antiquities* close to the end of the first century. Josephus gives a favorable notice to John the Baptist, although he does not connect him to Jesus. His account at least confirms the Gospel portrayal of John as a prophetic figure, as a baptizer, and as a martyr under Herod (*Antiquities* 18.5.2). When Josephus recounts the death by stoning of James at the hands of the Sanhedrin during the interregnum between the prefects Festus and Abinus, he identifies him as "the brother of Jesus who was called Christ" (*Antiquities* 20.9.1). The note confirms both the importance that Paul and Acts ascribe to James in the Jerusalem church in the middle of the first century, and his special relationship to Jesus described also in New Testament sources. It also connects the title *Christ* to the figure of Jesus.

A final passage in Josephus, the so-called *Testimonium Flavianum* (*Antiquities* 18.3.3), devotes a full paragraph to Jesus. The passage clearly contains Christian interpolations, and many critical scholars formerly regarded the entire passage as spurious. Recent scholarship, however, while recognizing the addition of sentiments impossible for Josephus to hold, has been more favorably disposed toward the hypothesis that the passage contains the nucleus of a passage about Jesus written by Josephus himself. It appears in a section of his text dealing with the way in which Pilate behaved badly in response to popular Jewish desires.

> At this time there appeared Jesus, a wise man, *if indeed one should call him a man*. For he was a doer of startling deeds, a teacher of people who receive the truth with pleasure. And he gained a following both among many Jews and among many of Greek origin. *He was the Messiah*. And when Pilate, because of an accusation made by the leading men among us, condemned him to the cross, those who had loved him previously did not cease to do so. *For he appeared to them on the third day, living again, just as the divine prophets had spoken of these and countless other wondrous things about him*. And up until this very day the tribe of Christians, named after him, has not died out.

Stripped of its obvious Christian accretions (indicated here by italics), the passage tells us a number of important things about Jesus, from the perspective of a first-century Jewish historian. Josephus asserts that Jesus was both a teacher and a wonder-worker, that he got into trouble with some of the leaders of the Jews, that he was executed under the prefect Pontius Pilate, and that his followers continued to exist at the time of Josephus's writing.

References to Jesus in other Jewish sources, such as the Babylonian Talmud, are far less reliable. They are, first of all, from a much later period, although some may derive from a time considerably earlier than that of the final composition of the Talmud in the fifth to sixth century. Second, references to Jesus and Christians have been subject to medieval censorship. Third, the Talmud's way of dealing with opponents was either to ignore them or to treat them in an oblique and coded fashion. Consequently, it is not always possible to detect, at this distance, precisely who or what the Talmud is opposing.

What is most valuable to the historian in the few passages that can be culled with confidence is the Talmud's obvious hostility toward Jesus. When, despite this bias, it confirms some element found also in other sources, the Talmud's testimony takes on greater worth. Thus, the talmudic passages that suggest a sexual scandal surrounding Jesus' mother (e.g., *Sanhedrin* 106a) obliquely support the Christian tradition that the manner of Jesus' birth was irregular. The most important talmudic passage is found in *Sanhedrin* 43a. Although revealing considerable confusion in detail, the passage asserts that Jesus was "hanged" on Passover after a (more than fair) Jewish trial determined that he should be "stoned" for "leading the people astray" into "apostasy" (which seems to suggest a teaching activity) and for "sorcery" (which suggests wonder-working activity).

Several early Greco-Roman sources focus primarily on Christians as such without explicit attention to Jesus. Thus, in his mention of the expulsion of the Jews from Rome under Claudius, the early-second-century historian Suetonius knows only that the turmoil precipitating the expulsion was "at the instigation of Chrestus" (*Life of Claudius* 25.4). The precious firsthand report of the governor of Bithynia, Pliny the Younger, to the emperor Trajan very early in the second century likewise focuses on the practices of the community, which includes singing hymns "to Christ as to a god" (*Letters* 10.96).

In contrast, the account of Nero's persecution of Christians after the fire in Rome given by the historian Tacitus (early second century) contains valuable evidence concerning Jesus: "Christus, from whom the name had its origin, suffered the extreme penalty during the reign of Tiberius at the hands of one of our procurators, Pontius Pilate, and a deadly superstition, thus checked for the moment, again broke out, not only in Judaea, the first source of the evil, but also in the city, where all things hideous and shameful from every part of the world meet and become popular" (*Annals* 15.44.2–8).

Tacitus is decidedly not positive, but his designation of the movement as a "superstition" is significant, for it locates Christianity specifically as a form of religiosity. The information that "Christus" (the outsider takes it as a proper name rather than a title) operated in Judaea and suffered the "extreme penalty" under Pontius Pilate during the reign of Tiberius agrees with Josephus and the Gospel accounts, but not in a way to suggest direct dependence: Tacitus does not explicitly use the term "crucifixion," for example, and does not connect Jesus to Judaism, or implicate Jewish leaders in his death as does Josephus. His statement that the movement was "checked" by Jesus' death but then "again broke out" can also be seen as a rough approximation, but from a negative perspective, of what the Christian narratives refer to as the resurrection experience.

Finally, Lucian of Samosata (ca. 120–180) wrote a satire on the Cynic philosopher Proteus Peregrinus that contains a fairly lengthy description of the Christians in Palestine, among whom Peregrinus sojourned for a time. Within his discussion, two parenthetical remarks are devoted to Jesus. The first refers to him as the one "whom they still worship, the man who was crucified in Palestine because he introduced this new cult into the world." The second says, ". . . their first lawgiver persuaded them that they are all brothers of one another after they have transgressed once for all by denying the Greek gods and by worshipping that crucified sophist himself and living under his laws" (*The Passing of Peregrinus* 11–13). These remarks are all the more intriguing because, beneath the note of contempt and outsider bias, they clearly place Jesus as a teacher ("sophist") and "lawgiver" in Palestine, connected to the Jewish traditions that reject polytheism, crucified (with Lucian twice using a term, not found in the Gospels, that means "impaled"), and now the object of cultic worship.

These are all the notices concerning Jesus from outsiders that can arguably be said to rely on observation, rumor, and reports rather than on the direct reading of the New Testament writings themselves. In the late second century, the massive attack on Christianity launched by the neoplatonic philosopher Celsus in his *True Word* explicitly relied not only on the Gospels but also on Jewish polemical writings available to him.

The earliest outsider reports contain considerable divergence, but there are also points of convergence. There is the appearance of the title *Christos* as a virtual name (Josephus, Suetonius, Tacitus, Pliny), his location in Palestine/Judaea (Josephus, bT *Sanh.* 43a, Tacitus, Lucian), his death by execution (Josephus, Tacitus, bT *Sanh.* 43a, Lucian), and the continued presence of a movement carrying his "name" (Josephus, Suetonius, Tacitus, Pliny, Lucian).

Less well attested is the placement of his death under Pontius Pilate (Tacitus, Josephus) or Tiberius (Tacitus) and the involvement of Jewish leaders in his death (Josephus, bT *Sanh.* 43a). In terms of Jesus' activities before his death, the only points of convergence are that he worked wonders (Josephus, bT *Sanh.* 43a) and that he was a teacher (Josephus, bT *Sanh.* 43a, Lucian).

Of equal importance to this positive evidence is what these sources do *not* say about Jesus and his movement. There is no trace of evidence that either he or the movement associated with him was identified as a political or military movement. And although Jesus' own activities could make him capable of being designated as a kind of "philosopher" or "sorcerer," the movement connected to him was not seen, by its first observers, either as a philosophy or as a form of magic, but rather in terms of religious categories: it was a depraved "superstition" (Suetonius, Tacitus, Pliny) or "cult" (Lucian).

NON-NARRATIVE NEW TESTAMENT EVIDENCE

Good historical method would seem to indicate as a next step considering what evidence there might be about Jesus in New Testament writings other than the Gospels. In particular, the letters of Paul present themselves as an obviously important source of information. His letters are, after all, our earliest datable extant Christian writings, and as non-narrative compositions that do not have Jesus' ministry as their explicit focus, whatever information they might contain about Jesus would seem to be of particular value.

One of the most shocking aspects of the recent Historical Jesus books, in fact, is their complete neglect of this Pauline evidence. It is noteworthy, for example, that *The Five Gospels* does not rank Jesus' flat prohibition of divorce any higher than a "gray," despite its clear divergence from the cultural norm and its being attested by Mark 10:10–12, Q (Matt. 5:32; 19:9; Luke 16:18), *and* Paul (1 Cor. 7:10).

The reasons for such avoidance of the Pauline evidence are not difficult to identify. For one thing, the recent Jesus books are explicitly committed to the model of Christian origins, discussed in the last chapter, that derives from Walter Bauer and states that diversity precedes unity. Diversity, however, has now come to mean something like complete separation. The Gospels are studied in total isolation from the Pauline letters, as though there were no links at all among the earliest Christian communities.

THE REAL JESUS

Not only Acts but also the evidence from Paul himself shows that such a compartmentalization is excessive and distorting. Paul reports that he went twice to Jerusalem, once three years after his calling to "report to Cephas" (Gal. 1:18), and again after fourteen years, when with the three leaders of the Jerusalem church he struck an agreement about the mission to the Gentiles (Gal. 2:7–9). He speaks of his own mission to the Gentiles, in fact, as extending "from Jerusalem to Illyricum" (Rom. 15:19), immediately before declaring his present intention to travel back to Jerusalem with his collection for the members of that community (15:25).

As for the content of his preaching, in 1 Corinthians 15:1–13, Paul insists that he proclaimed to his communities what he also had received, and that his preaching was in agreement with the other apostles: "Whether it was I or they, so we preach, and so you believed" (1 Cor. 15:11). The historian who wants to construct a version of Christian origins on a basis totally other than this must actively suppress Paul's own explicit declarations.

Some recent scholars have not been reluctant to see all such statements by Paul as reflecting his own self-aggrandizing lust for power. In sharp contrast to the century of scholarship that made Paul the hero at the beginning of the Christian movement, more recent tendencies have regarded Paul not only as the inventor of Christianity in its present, canonical form, but also as its "perverter" from the pristine message of Jesus. It is Paul who compromised the radical itinerant mission of Jesus with the urban realities of Greco-Roman culture; Paul who suppressed the female prophets who continued the gender-inclusive mission of the "woman-defined man," Jesus, and turned Christianity back to traditional patriarchalism; Paul who knew nothing of the countercultural Cynic teacher Jesus, but furthered the Hellenistic cult of the Son of God. The ideological commitment of such critics may lead them to prefer their image of Jesus to their image of Paul, but ideology makes for poor historical method.

Such a separation of Paul and Jesus actually represents a return to the perspective of an earlier generation, which saw Jesus as a "simple preacher" and Paul as the "genius" who invented Christianity. Thus, Paul's declaration in 2 Corinthians 5:16 ("even though we once regarded Christ according to the flesh, we no longer regard him that way") is taken as expressing an active *dis-*

interest in Jesus' life, if not a theological antipathy toward it. Paul's statement, however, in all likelihood refers to Paul's pre-call perception of Jesus, before his experience of the resurrected Lord. The best work done on Paul in recent years has demonstrated that Paul was not the inventor of the "Christ cult" but was, rather, the inheritor of liturgical and creedal traditions already in place before his conversion, which he received by means of human tradition.

Paul is certainly far from hostile toward the human person Jesus. He says in 1 Corinthians 12:3, ". . . no one speaking by the Spirit of God ever says 'Jesus be cursed!'" Paul's fundamental purpose is not, however, a retracing of the story of Jesus in the past. His concern is the replication of the *pattern* of that story—what he calls "the mind of Christ" (1 Cor. 2:16) or "the law of Christ" (Gal. 6:2)—in his communities (see Phil. 2:5). But the evidence best supports the position that Paul both knew and used elements from a narrative understanding of Jesus, shared by himself and his readers, to help him in this task.

First, Paul asserts that Jesus was born in human fashion, that he was Jewish, and that his mission was to the Jews when he declares, "God sent forth his son, born of a woman, born under the law, to redeem those who were under the law" (Gal. 4:4). Similarly, he states in Romans 15:8, "Christ became a servant to the circumcised to show God's faithfulness to the Patriarchs." Second, Paul considers Jesus to be "descended from David according to the flesh" (Rom. 1:3), a conviction found also in 2 Timothy 2:8, as well as in the Gospel narratives. Third, it is highly likely that Paul and his readers shared the tradition that Jesus prayed to God with the diminutive Aramaic form of *Abba* (see Gal. 4:6; Rom. 8:15–16).

Fourth, Paul refers to the authoritative words of Jesus concerning divorce (1 Cor. 7:10), payment for preaching (1 Cor. 9:14; see also 1 Tim. 5:17), and the end-time (1 Thess. 4:15). Fifth, Paul explicitly quotes the words of Jesus over the bread and the cup "on the night when he was betrayed" and identifies these words as a tradition received by him and passed on to his readers (1 Cor. 11:23–25). Sixth, Paul connects the death of Jesus to the Passover celebration of the Jews: "Christ our Paschal Lamb has been sacrificed" (1 Cor. 5:7). Seventh, Paul connects the death of Jesus to a condemnation by earthly rulers: "none of the rulers of this age understood this; for, if they had, they would not have crucified the Lord of glory" (1 Cor. 2:8). In 1 Timothy 6:13, a trial scene is made explicit: ". . . Christ Jesus, who in testimony before Pontius Pilate made the good confession."

Eighth, Paul's allusion to Psalm 69:9 in Romans 15:3 suggests that Jesus underwent abuse and humiliation: "For Christ did not please himself; but, as it is written, 'The reproaches of those who reproach thee fell on me.'" Ninth, if 1 Thessalonians 2:14–16 is authentic, and not an interpolation as some scholars hold, then Paul also involves the Jews of Judaea directly in the death of Jesus: ". . . the Jews, who killed both the Lord Jesus and the prophets, and drove us out, and displease God and oppose all men by hindering us from speaking to the Gentiles." It is certainly possible to object to this statement on theological grounds, but as historical evidence for a messianist's view of the death of Jesus about A.D. 50, it is difficult to wish away.

Tenth, Paul provides copious evidence that Jesus' manner of death was by crucifixion (1 Cor. 1:23; 2 Cor. 13:4; Phil. 2:8; Gal. 3:1). Eleventh, Paul attests to Jesus' having been buried (1 Cor. 15:4; Rom. 6:4). Twelfth, Paul asserts the reality of the resurrection, not simply as a conviction, but as an experience of visions or encounters testified to by many (1 Cor. 15:4–7), including himself (1 Cor. 9:1; 15:8; Gal. 1:15–16).

These Pauline statements occur outside a narrative framework. We would not recognize them as part of a "story" without extant narratives where they also occur. Paul's allusions are scattered and do not place the elements in the sequence I have provided, which is obviously that of the Gospel accounts. But for that very reason, they provide valuable external verification for points in the narratives we do possess. What sort of verification? Not that these things really happened, but that Paul assumed the readers of his letters, written within twenty to thirty years of Jesus' death, had already been taught that these things had happened. These bits of information in Paul do not prove the historicity of the events, but they confirm the antiquity and ubiquity of the traditions concerning the events, in a period as much as two decades earlier than our earliest written Gospel. I want to emphasize the term *ubiquity* as much as *antiquity*. Paul can assume, in other words, that the Roman church, which he had never met, had as firm a possession of these basic aspects of the Jesus story as did his own Corinthian community.

Other New Testament literature contains material pertinent to the Gospel accounts concerning Jesus. The Letter to the Hebrews, for example, also asserts that Jesus was Jewish and a descendant of Abraham (Heb. 2:14–16), and specifically descended from the tribe of Judah (Heb. 7:14; see Rev. 5:5; Luke 3:33); that he was tested and suffered (Heb. 2:18) and cried out in prayer to be saved from death "in the days of his flesh" (Heb. 5:7); that he died by crucifixion (Heb. 12:2) "outside the gate" of the city (Heb. 13:12). There is no reason to date Hebrews any later than the letters of Paul. Its information concerning Jesus confirms these points in the Gospel accounts, but does not in the least suggest literary dependence on those accounts (compare, e.g., Heb. 5:7–10 and Mark 14:32–35).

The Letter of James also, according to the majority of scholars who have carefully worked through its text in the past two centuries, is among the earliest of New Testament compositions. It contains no references to events in Jesus' life, but it bears striking testimony to Jesus' words. Jesus' sayings are embedded in James's exhortations in a form that is clearly not dependent on the written Gospels (see, e.g., James 1:5, 6, 12, 22–25; 2:5, 13, 14–16; 3:10–13; 4:8, 10; 5:9, 12). Other possible connections to Gospel materials are located in 1 Peter, 2 Peter, and Revelation. But since the dating of these compositions is far more debatable, they will not be considered here.

To summarize what this survey has yielded, I list here the points about Jesus made by New Testament writings other than the Gospels. Those points also shown to be attested in non-Christian writings are marked with an asterisk.

1. Jesus was a human person (Paul, Hebrews)*
2. Jesus was a Jew (Paul, Hebrews)*
3. Jesus was of the tribe of Judah (Hebrews)
4. Jesus was a descendant of David (Paul)
5. Jesus' mission was to the Jews (Paul)*
6. Jesus was a teacher (Paul, James)*
7. Jesus was tested (Hebrews)
8. Jesus prayed using the word *Abba* (Paul)
9. Jesus prayed for deliverance from death (Hebrews)

10. Jesus suffered (Paul, Hebrews, 1 Peter)
11. Jesus interpreted his last meal with reference to his death (Paul [by implication in Tacitus and Josephus])
12. Jesus underwent a trial (Paul)*
13. Jesus appeared before Pontius Pilate (Paul)*
14. Jesus' end involved some Jews (Paul)*
15. Jesus was crucified (Paul, Hebrews, 1 Peter)*
16. Jesus was buried (Paul)
17. Jesus appeared to witnesses after his death (Paul)

The most striking omission from this list is any mention of Jesus' wonder-working, which was attested by Josephus and the Talmud. The reason may be that the New Testament epistolary literature's focus is on the "signs and wonders" worked through the power of the Holy Spirit ("in the name of the Lord") in the present community, rather than on those worked by Jesus in the past (see, e.g., Rom. 15:19; Gal. 3:5; 2 Cor. 12:12; Heb. 2:4). It is also noteworthy that the largest number of these points clusters around the final part of Jesus' story. To repeat, non-narrative New Testament writings datable with some degree of probability before the year 70 testify to traditions circulating within the Christian movement concerning Jesus that correspond to important points within the Gospel narratives. Such traditions do not, by themselves, demonstrate historicity. But they indicate that memories concerning Jesus were in fairly wide circulation. This makes it less likely that the corresponding points in the Gospels were the invention of a single author or group. If that were the case, then such invention would have to be early enough and authoritative enough to have been widely distributed and unchallenged across the diverse communities with which Paul dealt. Such a hypothesis, of course, would work *against* the premise that Paul's form of Christianity had little to do with those interested in shaping the memory of Jesus.

PATTERNS IN THE GOSPELS

As I have tried to show, the character of the Gospel narratives does not allow a fully satisfying historical reconstruction of Jesus' ministry. Nevertheless, certain fundamental points on which all the Gospels agree, when taken together with confirming lines of convergence from outsider testimony and non-narrative New Testament evidence, can be regarded as historical with a high degree of probability. Even the most critical historian can confidently assert that a Jew named Jesus worked as a teacher and wonder-worker in Palestine during the reign of Tiberius, was executed by crucifixion under the prefect Pontius Pilate, and continued to have followers after his death. These assertions are not mathematically or metaphysically certain, for certainty is not within the reach of history. But they enjoy a very high level of probability.

Still other historical assertions can be made with only slightly less probability: that Jesus' mission was among his fellow Jews, for example, and that some Jews were involved in his death; or that Jesus initiated some sort of movement within Judaism by the gathering of followers. As we try to push beyond these broad (though extremely important) affirmations, the level of probability must necessarily decrease.

A reminder of what we mean by historical "probability" is appropriate here. The term refers to the degree of confidence we can have in *the state of our knowledge*. It does not adjudicate the "reality" of an occurrence or event but only what we can know of an occurrence or event. Historical probability rests upon the ability to verify statements by means of evidence or logic. Thus, I personally hold everything I have just stated about Jesus to be "certain," in the sense that I am intellectually convinced that these assertions correspond to reality. But *as a historian*, I can only state them as more or less probable, on the basis of the evidence available for verification.

The same method of convergence can suggest a fairly high degree of historical probability for other aspects of Jesus' ministry as reported in the Gospels. Thus, the pervasive testimony throughout the Gospel traditions that Jesus worked wonders corresponds to the suggestion in Josephus and the Talmud that he was a thaumaturge. Likewise, the outsider perception of Jesus as a teacher or sage corresponds to a wealth of sayings material in all the Gospels. Other broad patterns, such as the tradition that Jesus associated with those who were not "righteous" according to the norms of Torah, are so well attested at every level of the Gospel tradition that they can be said to have rather high historical probability.

Perhaps slightly lower on this scale, but likewise enjoying some substantial level of probability, are elements of the tradition such as that Jesus preached the kingdom of God, that he spoke in parables, and that he freely and idiosyncratically interpreted Torah. In all these cases, the weight of the testimony, in my judgment, tilts the burden of proof to the denial that Jesus acted in these ways.

Up to this point, I have identified only broad *patterns,* that is, assertions having to do with characteristic activities rather than specific incidents or sayings. The historian's job gets much more difficult when attention is given to the *pieces* within those patterns, to specific and concrete events. The criteria for making such determinations, as I have pointed out earlier, also inevitably become more circular and suspect.

Some cases are easier than others. As many scholars have argued, for example, it is highly probable that Jesus was baptized by John. The reasons for high probability in this case are simply stated: (1) John is described as a baptizer and preacher by Josephus; (2) the independence of his baptizing movement is also attested by John 3:22–30 and by Acts 18:24 and 19:3–7; (3) the redaction of the baptism scene in Matthew and Luke and its oblique treatment by John show that these evangelists were slightly embarrassed by the event; (4) the reasons for such embarrassment? The implication that John was superior to Jesus, or that Jesus was in need of repentance from sin. The combination of these factors suggests that there was every reason for the Gospels to suppress the event if they could, and therefore argues for its historicity.

Other cases are difficult but possible. It is quite conceivable and perhaps even likely that Jesus created an incident in the Temple; the timing and the meaning of that incident, however, are harder to state with the same degree of probability. Still others are even more difficult. It is easier to state in general that Jesus spoke in parables, for example, than to certify which ones come directly from him, or to determine their original form. Still other events escape the historian altogether, such as the transfiguration and the stilling of the storm.

At this juncture, a very basic point needs to be made about the "historical" character of such individual elements. The patterns and pieces alike, without the framework provided by a sustained narrative, must remain as discrete items—things that "Jesus said and did." It is *not* legitimate on the basis of demonstrating the probability of such items to then connect them, arrange them in sequence, infer causality, or ascribe special significance to any combination of them. This is why the abandonment of the Gospel narratives throws open the door for any number of combinations. Once that narrative control is gone, the pieces can be (and have been) put together in multiple ways. As I have pointed out in my review of Crossan and Borg, they have replaced the narrative control of the Gospels with the theoretical controls provided by anthropological models.

I have tried to show, by the method of converging lines of evidence, that *some* such combinations simply do not work. But that still leaves others possible. My point is, however, that whether plausible or implausible, all such constructions lack any real claim to historical probability once the given narrative framework has definitively been abandoned. The impact of this observation is less obvious for the end of Jesus' ministry. The support for the mode of his death, its agents, and perhaps its coagents, is overwhelming: Jesus faced a trial before his death, was condemned, and was executed by crucifixion.

But what about events before his arrest, trial, and death? Even if we determined on the basis of various criteria that Jesus "created an incident in the Temple"—as I think we can—we are not thereby allowed, without the synoptic framework, to place that event at the end of his ministry. Perhaps, as in John, it happened at the start of his public ministry. Still less can we legitimately deduce that this incident was the precipitant for Jesus' arrest, trial, and execution. Such is the sequence and connection provided by the synoptic narrative framework. But once we have abandoned it in principle—choosing to regard the evangelists as putting the "pieces" together out of literary and religious concerns rather than historical ones—we cannot then turn about and appeal to it when it suits.

A final example. I have argued that it is historically highly probable that Jesus was baptized by John in the Jordan. Fair enough. But from that fact, we cannot go on to state or assume that the baptism took place at the beginning of Jesus' ministry. We tend to assume that it happened then because that's where the Gospels place it. The Gospel narratives, furthermore, treat it as an initiation or messianic anointing, just as Christians subsequently used their baptism as an initiation ritual. Finally, the Synoptics remove John the Baptist from the scene after that incident, to present Jesus in an independent ministry.

But if we abandon the Gospels' narrative framework, what real reason do we have for placing the baptism at the beginning of Jesus' ministry? What reason do we have for thinking of it in terms of a point of transition between John's career and Jesus' own? The placement *and* the meaning of the event are given by the narrative, and if we abandon the narrative we have no reason to place it here rather than there, or to make any statements about what the event might have meant for Jesus.

It may be helpful to clarify my point. I actually have no doubts concerning the historicity of Jesus' baptism by John, and I think its meaning was probably what the Synoptics give it. I think it is logical for the baptism to have taken place at the start of Jesus' public ministry and that it probably did. But, I assert, there are no other *historical* grounds for determining its placement or meaning than those given by the Gospels themselves. Without their framework, we have only a fact, without context, without meaning.

Pushing Past the Framework

The chapter is entitled, "What's Historical About Jesus?" I have shown that the evidence is sufficient to support a substantial number of historical assertions concerning Jesus with a rather high degree of probability. We not only know that Jesus existed as something more than a fictional character—the sheer production of ancient literature interpreting him and referring to him suffices to show that—but we can have confidence about such fundamental issues as the time and place of his activity and the manner of his death, as well as some clues as to the character of his activity.

Certainly, we possess enough evidence to locate Christian religious claims in extramental and extratextual "reality." The evidence supports the position that Jesus was not the figment of someone's imagination, or a code word for a mushroom cult. Jesus was a real human person of first-century Palestine who was executed by crucifixion. We can go further and state that the basic "historical" claims of the Nicene Creed are well supported: "He was born of the virgin Mary, suffered under Pontius Pilate, was crucified, died, and was buried." The notable exceptions are the characterization of Jesus' mother as a "virgin" and his conception as being "of the Holy Spirit." Such claims could hardly be proved or disproved by historical analysis. The same disclaimer must be made about the creed's subsequent statements concerning the resurrection. The "historical" character of these is arguable, as I will try to show at the end of this chapter. But in essence, what the most universally used Christian creed asserts about the human person Jesus is historically verifiable.

Every quest of the historical Jesus begins to have credibility problems when scholars try to push beyond this framework. Just as with the analysis of early Christian development, historical method can here very easily become a form of madness, as data is pushed beyond its capacity to serve as genuine evidence. As with that case as well, the problem centers on the lack of genuine controls. Once one begins with the recognition that the Gospel narratives are not constructed according to principles of chronology or causality, then the various elements in the story become free-floating "pieces" that can be rearranged according to whatever principle or grid or structure is imposed on them.

In the first two chapters of this book, I criticized a number of Historical Jesus books for their sensationalism, speculativeness, and specious reasoning. The problem of pushing past the framework is real, however, even when carried out with the utmost sobriety and seriousness. A good illustration is provided by John P. Meier's *A Marginal Jew: Rethinking the Historical Jesus* (2 vols.; Doubleday, 1991, 1994). The first volume, *The Roots of the Problem and the Person*, has 484 pages; the second, *Mentor, Message and Miracle*, has 1,055 pages. Meier anticipates a third volume. His readers anticipate he may need even more.

There is nothing flashy or idiosyncratic about Meier's project. In fact, he deliberately sets himself the task of providing a consensus view. He begins his first volume with the fantasy of Jewish, Protestant, Catholic, and agnostic scholars being locked in the Harvard Divinity School library until they come to an agreement on what the historian can say about Jesus (1:1–2). Meier also recognizes that the "historical Jesus" should not be confused with the "real Jesus." The historical Jesus is but a reconstruction based on available evidence (1:21–40). Historical reconstructions, he also repeatedly recognizes, are fragile and have to do with what is probable rather than what is certain (2:340, 682, 778).

In contrast to the other books I have surveyed, Meier takes into account all the Jewish and Greco-Roman testimonies concerning Jesus (1:41–166), and is skeptical of the historical value of extracanonical gospels. He basically works with the four canonical Gospels, which he thinks offer the historian the best chance at a genuinely historical picture of Jesus. Like Borg and Crossan, however, Meier also brackets the Gospels' narrative framework in favor of an analysis of the separate pieces of tradition, which are subjected to the sort of criteria (multiple attestation, dissimilarity, coherence) generally employed for this sort of analysis (1:165–201).

Meier's treatment, in short, is as solid and moderate and pious as Historical Jesus scholarship is ever likely to be. More important, Meier is a careful scholar. There is nothing hasty or slipshod in his analysis; he considers every opinion, weighs every option. Precisely his enormous erudition, his self-conscious methodology, and his careful application of that methodology to specific cases, however, make his work the perfect example to illustrate the problems of pushing past the framework established by converging lines of evidence.

In his first volume, Meier reconstructs what can be known concerning Jesus' origins, family, language, and social status, using cross-cultural evidence sparingly but effectively (1:206–371). He then considers issues pertaining to the chronology of Jesus' ministry (1:372–443). In the second volume, he turns more directly to that ministry, considering in turn Jesus' relationship to John the Baptist ("Mentor"), Jesus' message concerning the future and inbreaking kingdom of God ("Message"), and Jesus' wonder-working ("Miracle").

Two aspects of his analysis deserve particular attention. The first is that his argument for the eschatological dimension to the mission of both John and Jesus stands in stark contrast to the tendency (found in the Jesus Seminar, Borg, and Crossan) to eliminate the eschatological from Jesus' ministry in favor of the image of a (only slightly Jewish) Cynic philosopher. In my view, Meier gives a better account of the evidence. Second, the five hundred pages of his second volume that he devotes to the traditions concerning Jesus the miracle worker are a useful counterbalance to scholars (in this case, *excluding* Borg and Crossan) who find such traditions embarrassing.

Meier's quest is for those pieces of the Gospel narratives that can, by the strict canons of scientific inquiry, be verified with a high degree of probability.

His approach is to locate the pieces that best satisfy all the criteria—and thereby can be considered on their own terms to be most "probable"—and then to argue outward to other pieces in search of a "pattern." By this means, for example, he concludes that it is probable in the highest degree that John the Baptist was a significant religious figure in first-century Palestine in his own right (confirmed by the New Testament as well as by Josephus), that he exercised a ministry of baptism, and that—with somewhat lesser probability—he proclaimed an eschatological message. Meier also thinks it highly probable that Jesus was baptized by John. The connections between these points, however, and their possible significance are much harder to establish in strictly historical terms.

We can observe in Meier's careful consideration of individual sayings, or specific actions, just how slippery and subjective the so-called criteria for historicity really are. Determining whether a tradition is "multiply attested" is relatively easy, and my own principle of "converging lines of evidence" is really just a version of that criterion. But the application of principles such as "dissimilarity" (or for Meier, "discontinuity") is extraordinarily difficult. This principle states that something can be attributed with probability to Jesus if it is dissimilar both to the cultural context of Judaism from which Jesus emerged and to the early church. In the strictest sense, the criterion demands what cannot be supplied, namely, a complete account of Jesus' Jewish context and a complete account of early Christian tradition, as a frame against which to measure a specific saying or event. Since the criterion cannot be applied strictly, its invocation often involves a considerable amount of special pleading and guesswork.

The same thing applies to the criterion of "embarrassment." One can readily agree in principle that the early church would be unlikely to invent something about Jesus that was offensive to it, but the application of the principle in specific instances once more demands access to early Christian sensibilities that the evidence does not allow. I have suggested that the application of this principle is useful in the case of the baptism of Jesus, precisely because there are converging lines of several types of evidence. When such convergence is not possible, the use of the criterion becomes more arbitrary and subjective.

As Meier moves from broad patterns to specific incidents, the sort of circularity involved in such demonstrations becomes more apparent, and the process of demonstration itself becomes less credible. In one sense, the very fairness and capaciousness of his discussions do some damage to his overall argument. As he offers objections to his views and rebuts them, the reader sometimes feels like a juror in a long trial, subject to endless examination and cross-examination, redirect and recross, and so on, so that the very process tends to obscure rather than clarify.

As he moves from the demonstration concerning specific pieces to the larger patterns, furthermore, Meier begins to draw some false inferences, manifesting symptoms of a condition that might be diagnosed as "creeping certitude." The main difficulty here, I think, is his frequent invocation of the "criterion of coherence," which holds that if by the rigorous application of all the other criteria we determine that Jesus did or said X, then other elements agreeing with X are also probable. The criterion seems to make a certain common sense. But common sense is not always logical. In fact, such an inference is illegitimate. For example, if it can be demonstrated with a high degree of probability that sometime in the past I baked a pumpkin pie, it cannot be inferred from this fact that I baked other pumpkin pies. Still less can it be inferred that I cooked other things, or loved cooking, or was a professional cook and baker. Likewise, if by using all the criteria we establish that one of Jesus' sayings spoke of a future kingdom of God, we cannot *on that basis* conclude that other future-kingdom-of-God sayings are more probable. It is theoretically possible that other such sayings were added by the tradition *on the basis* of that one authentic saying. This same observation can naturally be reversed: if we show that 90 percent of a certain family of sayings do come from the tradition rather than from Jesus, that conclusion does not in the least diminish the possibility of 10 percent of them being authentic.

To take this one step farther: if it can be demonstrated that Jesus did two different things, it is not therefore legitimate to understand those things in light of each other, as though they were mutually interpretive. The reason for this is clear: we lack knowledge of all the other things Jesus said and did that provide the only real context for the interpretation of specific deeds and sayings. It is historically *possible*, for example, that Jesus' exorcisms and his proclamation of the kingdom of God are connected (as the synoptic Gospels do connect them), but we cannot infer that connection, or state it as historically probable, simply from determining that Jesus both did exorcisms and proclaimed the kingdom of God. Another example (this time in response to Crossan rather than Meier): we might determine that Jesus *both* challenged the practices of the Temple in Jerusalem *and* invited people to an open table-fellowship, but we are not on that basis to use one of these facts to interpret the other. Why? Because we do not have the full range of deeds and sayings that could contextualize those separate facts. We only have the facts given to us by the Gospels *with* the connections they have suggested. I can illustrate again by extending the analogy used above: demonstrating that I *both* baked pies *and* taught students does not in the least demonstrate that I taught baking to students.

Such creeping certitude—not at all a condition unique to Meier—derives, I think, from the need to find patterns of meaning. The historian in the fullest sense is not content only with the what but above all with the why and the how of things. But if the narrative framework that has placed the pieces in a certain meaningful pattern has been abandoned, then the remaining pieces cannot by themselves form a new pattern. Anyone who has grappled with the *Gospel of Thomas* can testify to the difficulty of getting any real sense of "the meaning of Jesus" from that writing, precisely because of the disproportionate amount of "pieces" to "pattern" in it.

The determination of the historical probability of this item or that certainly does not enable the investigator to reach conclusions concerning intentions or inner motivation! But Meier does make such inferences: "Why, then, does Jesus choose this unusual phrase?. . . [it] indicates that he takes with utter seriousness the observation made above: the kingdom of God is simply a more abstract way of speaking of God as king" (2:298). Meier's making Jesus take seriously an observation in Meier's own book is only stylistic slippage. The more serious problem in the statement is that Meier's method does not enable him to deduce that Jesus "chose" a certain way of speaking because he took anything "with utter seriousness." Establishing the historical probability of a saying does not enable any conclusion concerning Jesus' options or opinions.

In another place, Meier says: "Nourished as he was on the Scriptures of Israel, Jesus was quite aware that God as creator had always been king" (2:299). His method, however, does not make it possible to reach knowledge of how "Jesus was aware." A final example: "We begin to see why Jesus was not interested in and did not issue pronouncements about concrete social and political reforms, either for the world in general or for Israel in particular" (2:331). Once more, Meier assumes access to Jesus' internal states of mind that no determination concerning a statement or deed could give. More than that, this final example also assumes information drawn from the Gospel narratives (concerning what reforms Jesus may or may not have enunciated), but not yet in any way established by Meier's own strict criteria of historicity (for other examples, see 2:316, 342, 349, 403, 453).

Using his method, Meier *is* able to identify those pieces of the Gospel narratives that can be argued with the highest level of probability to reach back to Jesus himself, or to traditions very close to Jesus himself. These pieces can be considered the "most certainly historical" elements in the Gospel narratives. But "most certain" in historiography always means simply "most probable." And even if we are able to determine pieces of the Gospel tradition that probably go back to Jesus, we are not *on that account* allowed to make inferences from such a *collection of facts* to the frequency, connectedness between, sequence, proportion, relative importance, and above all, the meaning of these facts.

This last point needs emphasis. That which can be verified historically is not at all necessarily what is most central or pivotal or essential to Jesus' ministry, any more than we can deduce from what is unique to a person what is essential or most important about that person. My having purple hair may (in climates other than the present one) make me unique, but I would hope it is not what is most important about me. Similarly, we may determine that Jesus said or did certain things, but it does not follow that these things that we can determine were more central or more *determinative of who Jesus was* than the things we cannot historically verify.

The synthetic picture of Jesus' ministry that Meier begins to advance in his second volume—that of an eschatological proclaimer of God's kingdom to Israel whose powerful deeds both announce and signify that divine rule—is, however true it might be, not strictly derivable from the methods that he himself has employed, and owes more than a little to the contribution made by the Gospel narratives that the method began by excluding.

Whether Jesus or Socrates, the most critical thing about a person is precisely what most eludes the methods of critical historiography, namely, the *meaning* of a character. One can show, therefore, that Jesus exorcized demons, spoke in parables, and declared the presence of God's rule, but *from this evidence* one could not say why he so acted, or what such deeds and words signified to him or to his followers. The problem is not the lack of data, but the inaccessibility of meaning. Meaning derives from the interpretation of the facts rather than the facts themselves. And such interpretation depends on story.

John Meier's achievement (as of this writing, still in progress) is to show, against theories that pretend to be critical but are not, and against the attempts to press the pieces into any number of dubious shapes, that several pieces of the Jesus tradition that the Gospel narratives themselves emphasize as important to the understanding of Jesus have a strong claim to historical probability. This is not a meager accomplishment.

It is important, however, to remind ourselves: things that can be determined to be historically probable are rendered neither more nor less *real* by that determination. Other things now unavailable to historical inquiry might have been just as real. All that is affected is the quality of our knowledge of those things. Our knowledge is not made greater, or better, or even more certain. It has simply become more "historical" in character. I repeat my caution not to equate historical with what is real, nor to equate historical knowing with all knowing. John Meier's great industry and erudition, impressive and admirable though they are, also suggest the limits of the methods that he shares with the other books we have considered.

History and the Resurrection

In the next chapter, I will argue that Christian faith has never—either at the start or now—been *based on historical reconstructions of Jesus,* even though Christian faith has always involved some historical claims concerning Jesus. Rather, Christian faith (then and now) is based on religious claims concerning the present power of Jesus.

Christianity in its classic form has not based itself on the ministry of Jesus but on the resurrection of Jesus, the claim that after his crucifixion and burial Jesus entered into the powerful life of God, and shares that life (whose symbol is the Holy Spirit) with those who can receive it. But before turning to that claim and its implications for the way in which the Gospels are read within the faith community, it is appropriate to consider here in some detail the way in which "the resurrection" can be considered "historical."

Definitions are of particular pertinence in this delicate case. Most important is grasping what the first Christians were claiming by "the resurrection experience." Missing this leads to considerable confusion. The best way to approach the subject is by negation. The resurrection is not a claim that Jesus did not die, although that peculiar view is attested in some apocryphal and Islamic texts. Christian and outsider texts alike attest to the reality of Jesus' death.

More significantly, the resurrection is not a claim that Jesus was resuscitated, that he resumed his former life after a "clinical death" experience. Such resuscitations are well documented both in ancient literature and today. Such were the revivals performed by Elijah on the widow of Sarepta's child (1 Kings 17:17–24), and by Jesus on Lazarus (John 11:17–44) and the widow of Nain's son (Luke 7:11–16). A resuscitation is excellent news for the patient and family. But it is not "good news" that affects everyone else. It does not begin a religion. It does not transform the lives of others across the ages. It is not what is being claimed by the first Christians.

The Christian claim concerning the resurrection of Jesus is not that he picked up his old manner of life, but rather that after his death he entered into an entirely new form of existence, one in which he shared the power of God and in which he could share that power with others. The resurrection experience, then, is not simply something that happened to Jesus but is equally something that happened to Jesus' followers. The sharing in Jesus' new life through the power of the Holy Spirit is an essential dimension of the resurrection. This power of new life, furthermore, is understood by Christians to be the basis for claiming that they are part of a new creation, and a new form of humanity shaped according to the image of the resurrected One. Paul draws the contrast best: "for as by a man came death, by a man also has come resurrection of the dead. For as in Adam all die, so also in Christ shall all be made alive . . . the first man, Adam, became a living being; the last Adam became a life-giving spirit" (1 Cor. 15:21–22, 45).

At the very heart of Christianity, therefore, is an experience and a claim. The experience is one of transforming, transcendent, personal power within communities that can be expressed in shorthand as "the gift of the Holy Spirit." The claim is that this power comes from Jesus, who was crucified but who now lives by the life of God, and is expressed by the declaration: "Jesus is Lord." Paul combines these in his statement: "No one can say 'Jesus is Lord' except by the Holy Spirit" (1 Cor. 12:3). Experience and conviction together form the primordial "resurrection experience" that founds the Christian movement and continues to ground it today. As Paul also says, "If Christ has not been raised, then our preaching is in vain, and your faith is in vain" (1 Cor. 15:14).

Although traditions about the empty tomb are ancient, they are not at the heart of the resurrection experience, for an empty tomb is simply a fact about the past that is compatible, as the Gospel of Matthew clearly shows, with a variety of explanations, including the theft of the body. More important, the absence of a body does not by itself empower a community. It is a new form of presence that needs explanation, not an absence.

In similar fashion, traditions concerning visions of Jesus are ancient and important (see 1 Cor. 15:3–8). But these encounters also, when closely read, show themselves to have as their point not so much the fact that Jesus was "alive" as it was the experience of Jesus "giving life," that is, empowering his followers to mission. The "Easter visions" give narrative expression to an experience that far transcended the encounters of select individuals. The resurrection experience that founded and that grounds the Church is not based on the transitory encounters of a few people on Easter day or for forty days thereafter, but on the experience of power through Jesus by generations of people across the centuries and continuing until today.

Whatever the character of the ministry of Jesus or the "Jesus movement" before his death, it is the experience of the transformed Jesus as Lord that begins the "Christian movement." The resurrection is the necessary and suffi-cient cause of the religious movement, as well as the literature that it gener-ated and that reveals everywhere the perception of Jesus given by the experience of his transforming power and the conviction that he "sits on the right hand of God" as Lord.

If this understanding of the resurrection is fair to the evidence in the New Testament, and I submit that it is, then in what sense can it be called "histori-cal"? If the resurrection were simply the matter of the empty tomb, then it would be "historical" in a straightforward way, though perhaps difficult to ne-gotiate. If the resurrection were a matter of visions and locutions of a dead per-son experienced by some followers, then it would be "historical" not as part of the history of Jesus but as part of the story of his followers, although once again hard for the historian to verify.

But if the resurrection means, as defined here, the passage of the human Jesus into the power of God, then by definition it is not "historical" as regards Jesus, in the sense of a "human event in time and space." By definition, the resurrection elevates Jesus beyond the merely human; he is no longer defined by time and space—although available to human beings in time and space! The Christian claim concerning the resurrection in the strong sense is simply *not* "historical." The problem in this case is, however, not with the reality of the resurrection. The problem lies in history's limited mode of knowing. Yet, to make one final turn, the resurrection of Jesus in this strong sense *can* be said to be "historical" as an experience and claim of human beings, then and today, that organizes their lives and generates their activities. That is, the resurrec-tion has a historical dimension as part of the "resurrection community" that is the Church.

I have tried to report faithfully my sense of what the New Testament writ-ings themselves understand by the resurrection, and what understanding of the resurrection must be held in order to comprehend the start of the Christian religion and the production of the New Testament. I hold that some sort of powerful, transformative experience is required to generate the sort of move-ment earliest Christianity was, and to necessitate the sort of literature the New Testament is (see also my *Writings of the New Testament: An Interpreta-tion* (Fortress, 1986, pp. 1–20, 87–140).

DIFFERENT UNDERSTANDINGS

My readers should be aware, however, that much of what I have stated goes against the grain of a great deal of contemporary New Testament scholarship. In the name of history, the synthetic understanding I have described has been fragmented in two ways.

Some argue that the understanding of the resurrection I have described is found only within certain streams in early Christianity. It is argued that other elements of Christianity (or the "Jesus movement") had no such experience or conviction concerning Jesus, yet had a certain "Christology" of their own based on Jesus' ministry of teaching and/or wonder-working, or based in the expectation that he would return as Son of man. One version of this view is found in Crossan: "Easter faith . . . started among those first followers of Jesus in Lower Galilee long before his death, and precisely because it was faith as empowerment rather than faith as domination, it could survive and, in fact, negate the execution of Jesus himself" (*Who Killed Jesus?* p. 209).

In this view, the "resurrection model" of Christianity eventually subsumed the other versions. Such an understanding obviously underlies Burton Mack's portrait of the Q community (see *The Lost Gospel* and *A Myth of Innocence*), but Mack's position regarding "Christian" communities existing apart from the resurrection faith is scarcely idiosyncratic, having been argued as well by the Catholic theologian E. Schillebeeckx in his *Jesus: An Experiment in Christology* (English translation; Crossroad, 1979).

Other scholars, also in the name of history, regard the strong version of the resurrection that I have presented as a later theological development (especially by Paul and John) and seek to find the "originating experience" of Christianity in "historical terms," that is, as just another human event in time and space. They tend to locate the resurrection entirely as an intrapsychic experience of followers. Fascinatingly, the key experience is usually attributed to Peter. For Bishop Spong (*The Resurrection*), the resurrection experience is something like a light bulb suddenly going on over Peter's head, when Peter realizes that God was in Jesus during his life: *that* realization, says Spong, that mental adjustment or insight, is the sufficient cause of a world religion. But again, Spong's view is not so different from that of the mainstream German New Testament scholar Willi Marxsen, who in his last book, *New Testament Foundations for Christian Ethics* (English translation; Fortress, 1993), defines the resurrection as just such an experience of Peter's that is communicated to others.

Because these positions are widely held, their deficiencies deserve attention. The first alternative view—that the resurrection experience was found only among some early Christians but not all—suffers from a lack of positive evidence. Certainly, the canonical New Testament writings as we now have them all assume the resurrection, including the Letter of James, whose Christology is minimal. The "opponents" who appear in various Pauline letters seem for the most part to hold if anything an exaggerated appreciation of the resurrection, rather than the opposite. Matthew and Luke-Acts have obvious and explicit grounding in the resurrection. Such diverse canonical witnesses as the Gospel of John, Hebrews, 1 Peter, and Revelation all have the same conviction, albeit with diverse understandings. The argument made by some that the Gospel of Mark knows nothing of the resurrection and hopes only for the triumphant return of Jesus at the *parousia* flies in the face of the Gospel's own literary signals. Some version of the resurrection is also a feature of noncanonical writings such as the *Gospel of Peter* and the various apocryphal Acts. The Gnostic writings from Nag Hammadi that are demonstrably Christian (such as the *Gospel of Thomas* and *Treatise on the Resurrection*) seem to have an understanding of the resurrection of Jesus that is distinctive, viewing it as a quality of his existence rather than a postmortem event, but they still assume that the resurrection is a central symbol that requires negotiation.

The claim that the resurrection was not a feature of all early Christian experience rests, so far as I can tell, largely on the reading of Mark's Gospel that I mentioned in the preceding paragraph, and the "recovery" of "primitive community beliefs" from the hypothetical Gospel source, Q. But the reification of this hypothetical source into a self-contained composition with its own theology is a highly doubtful enterprise. And, as I tried to show in chapter 2, the attempt of Burton Mack to use Q as the guide to a form of the "Jesus movement" in Galilee that had no contact with the resurrection experience is an exercise in baseless speculation.

The second alternative view—that the resurrection was merely a "vision" of Peter amounting to a mental adjustment—must answer to the question of evidence as well as that of logic. The evidence of the New Testament (and indeed of the apocryphal New Testament literature as well) is that the experience of the resurrection went far beyond the personal experience of one person. Our earliest testimony (1 Cor. 15:3–8) speaks not of an experience of Peter that was related to others, but of an experience that was had by many others in addition to Peter, including Paul himself. This understanding is, of course, that of the Gospel accounts as well, whose appearance accounts characteristically involve small groups of people rather than solitary individuals, and whose emphasis is consistently placed on the powerful mandate carried by the resurrected One's presence. In short, both the appearance accounts and Luke's Pentecost account stress, not the vagueness of an inner realization, but the forceful encounter with an Other.

The matter is also one of simple logic: for an effect, we need a necessary and sufficient cause. Anyone becoming aware of the drastically reduced number of Jews in Europe in 1945 compared with 1932 could logically posit a cause sufficient to account for that effect. Such reasoning would not necessarily lead to the specific description of the Holocaust. But it would necessarily lead to some force sufficiently great to accomplish so awesome an effect. Theories of increased tourism would not do. In the case of early Christianity, the explanation of this world religion's birth by a single person's hallucination (As E. Renan attributed to Mary Magdalen in his *Life of Jesus,* 1863), or "vision," or "realization," is simply incommensurate with the explosive character of the movement that within twenty-five years, under the most trying of circumstances, managed to create communities across the Mediterranean world. The same applies to A. Loisy's declaration that *faith* was resurrected on Easter (*The Birth of the Christian Religion,* 1933). The effort to reduce the resurrection experience to just another historical event runs the risk of failing to account for the rise of the historical movement. The *denial* of the resurrection experience poses an even greater problem of origination: if some such experience was not at the root of the movement, what accounted for its unlikely birth, amazing growth, and peculiarly tension-filled literature?

But can there be a "nonhistorical" event that has historical effects? Of course. It happens all the time, if seldom so dramatically as in the case of nascent Christianity. We can point not only to the examples of such religious founders as Muhammad and Siddhartha, whose own "formative/originative" experiences remain inaccessible on the historical plane, but also to the multiple instances of artists, and poets, and mystics, and lovers, and parents, whose "effects" are obvious and well known but whose "causes" remain inaccessible to historical inquiry.

Insistence on reducing the resurrection to something "historical" amounts to a form of epistemological imperialism, an effort to deny a realm of reality beyond the critic's control. That, however, is not even good history. It is instead an ideological commitment to a view of the world that insists on material explanations being the only reasonable explanations, that reduces everything to a flat plane where not even genius, much less the divine, can be taken into account. Such an ideological commitment begins with the assumption that Christianity *cannot* have anything distinctive about it.

For the responsible historian, however, the recognition of forces and realities beyond the ken of strict historical method is what makes the doing of history exciting and ennobling. When a so-called historian uses the historical method to deny, in effect, the reality of anything beyond what that method can demonstrate, we suspect a certain defensiveness to be at work. When such denial is practiced by someone also claiming to be a Christian, something still more curious is happening.

CHAPTER 6

The Real Jesus and the Gospels

The Jesus Seminar's promise to deliver, by means of historical methods, "the real Jesus" is, we have seen, fraudulent on two counts. The first is that its historical methodology is flawed. The second is that even the best historical reconstruction cannot supply "the real Jesus," any more than it can supply "the real Socrates." Historians can make a number of important, indeed critical, assertions about Jesus' ministry, but the evidence provided by the ancient sources does not enable a satisfying reconstruction of it.

More mischievous than the claim to reveal the "real Jesus" is the implication that historical reconstruction provides so fundamental a critique of Christian faith that the church needs to reexamine its creeds. If historical evidence is lacking that Jesus called himself the Messiah, the implication is that the church is wrong to think of him as Messiah. If historical criticism cannot demonstrate that Jesus predicted his return, the implication is that Christians are wrong in awaiting his triumphant coming. The assumption appears to be that what Jesus said and did and thought is the object of Christian faith. The most destructive effect of the Jesus Seminar and recent Historical Jesus books has been the perpetuation of the notion that history somehow determines faith, and that for faith to be correct, the historical accounts that gave rise to it have to be verifiable.

But this simply is not true. The first reason is the obvious one: historical reconstructions are by their very nature fragile and in constant need of revision. They cannot sustain the commitment of the human heart and life. Even the most casual survey of all the Jesus reconstructions offered just in the last twenty years, furthermore, discovers a bewildering variety of conflicting portraits of Jesus, and a distressing carelessness in the manner of arriving at those portraits. If historians cannot be pious at least about their own trade, why should their suggestions be taken as the guide to religious piety?

The second reason is that, although the Christian creed contains a number of historical assertions about Jesus, Christian faith as a living religious response is simply not directed at those historical facts about Jesus, or at a historical reconstruction of Jesus. Christian faith is directed to a living person.

The "real Jesus" for Christian faith is the resurrected Jesus, him "whom God has made both Lord and Christ" (Acts 2:36). And since Christians understand by the resurrection not simply a resuscitation of Jesus' body but his entry into God's own life (symbolized by his "enthronement at the right hand of God"—Acts 2:34), which is manifested in the powerful presence of the Holy Spirit among believers ("having received from the Father the promise of the Holy Spirit, he poured out this which you see and hear"—Acts 2:33), the *real Jesus* for Christian faith is not simply a figure of the past but very much and above all a figure of the present, a figure, indeed, who defines believers' present by his presence.

As these quotations from Peter's speech in Acts 2 indicate, Christians have always taken the resurrection to be the defining event concerning Jesus, and the fundamental perspective from which to perceive "the real Jesus." Whether Jesus declared himself to be the Messiah during his lifetime is irrelevant; by his resurrection, God has "made him both Lord and Messiah" (Acts 2:36). Whether Jesus predicted the *parousia* is irrelevant; it is because he lives now as powerful Lord that the Church expects him to inaugurate God's final triumph: "For since we believe that Jesus died and rose again, even so, through Jesus, God will bring with him those who have fallen asleep" (1 Thess. 4:14).

It is Jesus as risen Lord who is experienced in the assembly of believers, declared by the word of proclamation, encountered in the sacramental meal, addressed by prayers of praise and petition. It is "in the name" of *this* Jesus that powerful deeds of healing are performed. It is through the Spirit given by this glorious Lord that believers are able to express gifts of tongues and prophecy and teaching and service within the community and by the Spirit of freedom given by this Lord that they are themselves being transformed from glory to glory. So it was at the birth of the Christian faith, and so is it today wherever Christianity is spiritually alive and identifiably Christian in character.

The distinction I am making is of absolutely fundamental importance. Yet, even among Christians, the point of it is frequently missed. Repetition in this case, then, might be allowed: Christians direct their faith not to the historical figure of Jesus but to the living Lord Jesus. Yes, they assert continuity between that Jesus and this. But their faith is confirmed, not by the establishment of facts about the past, but by the reality of Christ's power in the present. Christian faith is not directed to a human construction about the past; that would be a form of idolatry. Authentic Christian faith is a response to the living God, whom Christians declare is powerfully at work among them through the resurrected Jesus.

The point can be made one more time, by an analogy (borrowed and adapted from Karl Rahner, "On the Development of Dogma"). The situation with the Christians' memory of Jesus is not like that of a long-ago lover who died and whose short time with us is treasured. The situation, rather, is like that of a lover who continues to live with the beloved in a growing and maturing relationship. In such a situation, the memory of the past is constantly affected by the continuing experience of the other in the present. For me (and I am sure, for my wife), the issue of where my wife and I had our first date, or realized we were in love, or even made our vows, is of much less significance to each of us than the issue of whether our love is alive and powerfully real now, in the present. Moreover, even though the love shown me by my wife is experienced as continuous with that she showed me in the early years of our relationship, in no way do I find that love *dependent* on the right interpretation of those earlier experiences. Our relationship is confirmed or disconfirmed not by settling the issue of who we were back then but by engaging the issue of who we will be together now. So also is the Church's memory of Jesus constantly affected by his continuous and powerful presence, and confirmed or disconfirmed by the reality of his presence.

The Identity of Jesus in the Gospels

From start to finish of the various quests for the historical Jesus, the four canonical Gospels have been regarded primarily as a problem to be overcome: they are written from the perspective of resurrection faith, and they offer divergent testimony. We have reviewed some of the strategies devised to overcome that problem. The first quest began by eliminating anything that smacked of the "miraculous," then chose the Synoptics as more reliable than John, then sorted through the Synoptics in search of the earliest and presumably least-corrupted version. The latest quest dismantles the narrative structure of the Gospels, putting all the separate pieces of tradition in a pile with all the similar pieces from the extracanonical gospels, then testing according to "criteria of historicity" for the pieces that go back to Jesus. The premise of the last search as for the first is: the only way to find "the real Jesus" is to bypass the Jesus found in the canonical Gospels.

The very thing that appears to such questers as the core problem, however, is seen by Christians as the best and truest aspect of the Gospels, namely, their postresurrection perspective. The Historical Jesus researchers insist that the "real Jesus" must be found in the facts of his life before his death. The resurrection is, when considered at all, seen in terms of visionary experience, or as a continuation of an "empowerment" that began before Jesus' death. Whether made explicit or not, the operative premise is that there is no "real Jesus" after his death.

Christians, when they are consistent with their own classical tradition, take the exact opposite position: the "real Jesus" is the one who is now alive and powerfully present, through the Holy Spirit, in the world and in the lives of human beings. The Gospels, therefore, provide access to the "real Jesus" precisely insofar as they reflect the perception of him given by his postresurrection existence.

From the perspective of Christian faith in the resurrected Lord, any claim to capture the "real Jesus" that stops short of his resurrection is as wildly wrongheaded as an insistence that a biography of Franklin Roosevelt could stop at Campobello, or that a life of Churchill would be more accurate if it stopped short of Dunkirk. The very things that made these figures of our century of historical importance, that is, their "life after" crippling injury and political death, would be left out by such a method.

Indeed, both authors and readers of such biographies search for intimations of later and public greatness in the early stages of such dramatic and influential characters. For a political life so filled with failure and frustration as Churchill's, the reader needs a reminder of the greatness in order to survive all the hardships that precede it. Thus, William Manchester's magisterial *The Last Lion* begins with an evocation of Dunkirk and the summoning of

Churchill to the prime ministership, before drawing the reader through the long, sad days of his childhood and adolescence. The reader's perspective from the start is established by the "great Churchill," for in retrospect, that was precisely the "real Churchill."

For those living in a community where "signs and wonders" done in the name of Jesus are a regular occurrence, hearing of such deeds attributed to Jesus in the Gospel narratives is no surprise or scandal. The modality of the wonder may be different or more subtle, but in every physical and emotional and spiritual transformation accomplished in the name of Jesus within the community, the same power of the resurrected One is recognized. The "truth" of the miracles in the Gospels, therefore, is something more than historical. The miracles told of Jesus reflect not only past but also present realities. They are existentially true, religiously true.

For those living in a community where the "Word of the Lord" proclaimed through preaching and prophecy is understood as the authoritative word of the resurrected One speaking through the Holy Spirit, a word to be received as authoritative and normative for life, it is no surprise or scandal to hear those same words attributed to Jesus in the Gospels, for it is the *same* Jesus who speaks in both places. The proclamation of God's rule, the call to discipleship, the demand for renunciation of possessions and power and family, the commandment of love for God and neighbor—these are not heard as the opinions of an ancient philosopher that can be entertained or not, but as the very Word of the Lord by which the community "led by the Spirit" must also "walk by the Spirit" (Gal. 5:25).

For a community that lives in the presence of the resurrected One, it is beside the point to debate whether Jesus "back then" predicted his death and resurrection, for his death and above all his resurrection are confirmed as real precisely by this community that lives by his power. It is equally silly, in this context, to debate whether Jesus "back then" predicted his return, for that return is predicated on his being the living and powerful Lord, and it is in the light of that truth that we await God's final triumph through him. When we read of the return of the Son of man placed in the mouth of Jesus in the

Gospels, therefore, we are not in the least worried about the "historical" basis for that statement. What is significant (for us now!) is the existential import of the statement: our life is lived under a certain judgment.

For a community of faith that lives in the presence of the resurrected One, it is absurd, even a betrayal of the truth, to consider the passion of Jesus "apart from" the interpretation of those events given by the Gospels, which from the beginning clothed his death in the garments of Torah. Precisely within this community, we find that it is "by his wounds that we have been healed" (1 Pet. 2:24; Isa. 53:5). Likewise, the parables of Jesus in the Gospels are not read within this community as though they encoded events of the past; they are read as speaking to realities of today. The parable of the lost sheep (Luke 15:3–7; Matt. 18:12–14) is understood not to be about events in the past but in the present, for "you were straying like sheep, but have now returned to the shepherd and guardian of your souls" (1 Pet. 2:25). The parables have existential rather than historical truth, for they depict the mystery of call and response to the Messiah who now lives. Thus, the community of faith finds no historical anachronism but rather the most pertinent and present religious truth in John 10:14–15: "I am the good shepherd; I know my own and my own know me, as the father knows me and I know the father; and I lay down my life for the sheep."

For such a community of readers—and I think I have fairly described the classical Christian understanding of the situation—any attempt to reconstruct a historical Jesus (as a norm for faith!) that did not take the resurrection into account as the most important reality about Jesus would be regarded as worse than impertinent and irrelevant. It would be regarded as a betrayal and as a lie. For a Christian community to base itself on such a reconstruction would be, in effect, to deny the power—that is to say, the reality—of the resurrection.

The Diversity and Unity of the Gospel Witness

So much for the "problem" of the resurrection perspective. The diversity in the canonical Gospels has also appeared to be a hindrance to a historical reconstruction of Jesus. Actually, that is not entirely the case, for, as I have shown, the obvious differences among these accounts make their points of convergence the more valuable for historical purposes. For the Christian community whose religious response is to the resurrected Lord rather than to a historical reconstruction, however, the diversity of the Gospel witness appears more as gift than as difficulty.

Some approximation to the "sense of the church" in this matter can be gained by reviewing some of the canonical decisions made by the church in response to options presented in the second century. These decisions make it clear that the Gospels, in all their diversity, were treasured for something other than their ability to render a historically accurate Jesus.

The first option was presented in the mid-second century by Marcion. His radically dualistic view of the world located evil in matter and goodness in spirit. The creator God presented by the Old Testament was therefore regarded as responsible for evil. Jesus did not represent this creator God but revealed instead a previously unknown God who had nothing to do with the creation and offered salvation from this material world. For Marcion, only Paul properly understood the good news. Even the other "Christian" writings were all deeply influenced by "Judaizers," who desired to drive Christianity back to the religion of the evil-creating and lawgiving God.

On the basis of these views, Marcion established a canon of Scripture smaller than the traditional one then already in the process of formation. It consisted of Paul's letters (minus the Pastorals) and the Gospel of Luke. Marcion thought Paul was referring to a written composition when he referred to "my gospel," and Luke, suitably purged of its Jewish elements, seemed in Marcion's view to best meet the standard of theological correctness. Marcion offered the option of a canon constituted by theological self-consistency. By its rejection of Marcion, the church asserted, by implication, that the canon can contain a legitimate theological diversity. The different perspectives of the Gospels therefore are to be valued precisely in their differences.

The second century offered a second option, this time presented by Tatian. Apparently scandalized by the plurality of the Gospels, Tatian composed the *Diatessaron* (literally, "through the four"), which wove together the four canonical versions into a single, consistent narrative. Tatian seemed to be assuming that a single "story of Jesus" should be normative for Christians. Although he worked completely with the canonical versions, Tatian's attempt to create a single seamless narrative was, in effect, the first "Life of Jesus" or "Historical Jesus." Tatian's work was enormously successful in some areas for several centuries. But even in those regions, it was eventually supplanted by the four Gospels it had been intended to replace. The rejection of Tatian's option represented the affirmation of the fourfold Gospels in all their factual diversity and disagreement. By implication, the Gospels are valued as witnesses to and interpretations of the "real Jesus," rather than as sources for the "historical Jesus."

In the light of these decisions, the response of Augustine to the attacks of the neoplatonic philosopher Porphyry several centuries later can be regarded as unfortunate, if thoroughly understandable. The situation in some ways anticipated the contemporary one. Porphyry's attack was directed specifically against the historical reliability of the Gospels, based, as so much later criticism was (see especially David Strauss), on the disparities and disagreements among the four canonical accounts. The impossibility of reconciling these versions at the historical level was taken as discrediting the Gospels as religious witnesses. Porphyry's assumption, of course, was that the value of their witness was *as* historical sources.

Augustine's response was to write *On the Harmony of the Gospels,* in which he undertook to demonstrate the fundamental agreement of the four Gospels on essential points. Augustine's effort was an impressive tour de force, and was undoubtedly motivated by the desire to defend the worth of the Gospels. It was, however, intellectually shortsighted. By seeking to ground the truth of the Gospels in historicity, he prepared the way for the much later critics who, operating with the same equation, would use the Gospels' nonhistoricity to challenge their truth.

What both Augustine and Tatian missed, and what the questers for the historical Jesus seem never to have grasped, is that the church canonized separate *literary compositions* called Gospels. These texts *as* texts are read in the assembly as the word of God, are debated in council for the direction of the church, are used in theology for the understanding of faith. By canonizing four such versions of gospel, the church obviously also accepted them in all their diversity *as normative.* That is to say, their normative character is not found *outside* these texts and apart from their diversity, but *within* these texts in all their diversity. Insofar, then, as an attempt is made to construct a normative picture of Jesus outside these texts and by eliminating their diversity, the effort is outside the framework of the church's canon, and contrary to its implied intention.

There are at least three positive implications of the church's canonization of the four Gospels as witnesses to and interpretations of Jesus in narrative form. The first is that the reality of Jesus, not only as risen Lord, but also in his hidden human manifestation of the divine presence, is richer and more complex than can be contained in any single version: Mark's presentation of Jesus as suffering Son of man, Matthew's portrayal of him as Lord and Teacher of the Church, Luke's image of Jesus as the Prophet like Moses, and John's interpretation of him as the Revelation of the Father—each of them, the church declares, is true in its fashion, and yet none of them captures all the truth.

The second implication is that the fourfold version of the gospel also symbolizes the infinite replicability of the story of Jesus in the lives of human beings. The story of Jesus is not simply past, the church declares, but continues as the Spirit of Jesus transforms the lives of human beings according to the "mind of Christ" (1 Cor. 2:26). But in what sense can the story of Jesus be replicated? Surely not in the specifics of his ministry, which are irretrievably past: his maleness, Jewishness, celibateness, beardedness, itinerancy. Such "historical" elements are not repeatable. But neither are they important to repeat.

This leads to the third implication: the plurality of the Gospels—above all at the level of such specific facts, the past of when and where—points beyond itself to a deeper significance, which is the *meaning* of the story of Jesus contained in these narratives. It is not the facts of Jesus' life that can find new expression in the lives of others, but rather the *pattern* of his existence. Jesus' existence as one of radical obedience toward God and self-disposing service toward others forms a pattern for all humanity that can be written in the heart by the Holy Spirit. It is this pattern that Paul designates as the *nomos Christou* ("the law of Christ," or, better, "pattern of the Messiah").

The second century—which truly was the pivotal period for Christian self-definition—also offered the church an opportunity to expand its repertoire of Gospels. A variety of gospels were produced, above all by the movement known as Gnosticism. The emphatic rejection of the Gnostic gospels sheds light on the limits of the canon's tolerance for diversity. It has become popular in some circles to attribute the process of canonization to purely political motivations or a fixed patriarchal ideology. A careful assessment reveals a more complex set of issues.

We notice first that in contrast to the canonical Gospels, the Gnostic gospels are conspicuously lacking in narrative structure. The *Gospel of Thomas* is a loose collection of sayings; the *Gospel of Philip* and the *Gospel of Truth* are rather more meditative or hortatory; the *Dialogue of the Savior* is a conversation between Jesus and his followers. The lack of narrative is, I think, not accidental, but corresponds to the deepest perceptions of the Gnostic movement. Narrativity, after all, inevitably involves materiality. To have the good news revealed in a human story represents an affirmation of the body and of time, which are intrinsically attached to materiality. No matter how diverse in detail, then, the narrative Gospels implicitly assert the compatibility of the material and spiritual orders, and therefore that God could work for salvation within the material world. But precisely that conviction is incompatible with the Gnostic perception of materiality as a ghastly error or malicious trick. The acceptance of narrative gospels, together with the rejection of non-narrative gospels, may not have been conscious or intentional on the part of the canonizers. But by this choice they asserted that the fundamental importance of "the earthly Jesus" lay not in the detailed historical facts of his existence—or in the truths that he revealed—but in the character of the human life he lived.

Even more strikingly, the Gnostic gospels lack passion accounts. The death of Jesus is either omitted or touched on only lightly. Their emphasis is on the revelation of the divine. In the canonical Gospels, as we have seen, the passion accounts play a central and climactic role. The emphasis of the canonical Gospels is on the suffering of the Messiah. The difference in emphasis might again be connected to perceptions of the compatibility of the divine with material reality. But more than that, it has to do with perceptions of how divine power works in the world. In Gnostic Christianity, the enlightenment of the mind enables the avoidance of suffering. In classical Christianity, the gift of the Holy Spirit leads one through the same path of suffering that was followed by the Messiah.

I said that the canonical Gospels view Jesus from the perspective of the resurrection. That is true. But in sharp contrast to the Gnostic gospels, which have *only* that perception, the canonical Gospels hold that vision of power in tension with the reality of Jesus' suffering and death. In each of the four canonical Gospels, Jesus is portrayed in terms of *kenosis*, or self-emptying. In none of the canonical Gospels is the scandal of the cross removed in favor of the divine glory. In each, the path to glory passes through real suffering. Despite all the diversity concerning the details of Jesus' ministry, the canonical Gospels agree on this fundamental *pattern*.

The Gospel and the Gospels

The Jesus Seminar and the recent Historical Jesus publications I have reviewed in this book tend to separate the Gospel materials from other New Testament writings. The effect of this divorcement has been the loss of important controls for statements concerning the historical Jesus: the writings of Paul, Hebrews, 1 Peter, and James contain a number of assertions about the ministry of Jesus that antedate the written Gospels and help to support discrete elements within them.

Another result of separating the Gospels from the rest of the New Testament is the freedom to impose *patterns* on the Gospel materials other than those given by the Gospel narratives themselves. If meaning derives above all from narrative, and if we remove the meaning of Jesus' ministry given it by the Gospels, we are simply left with a pile of pieces that must be reconstructed on the basis of some other pattern.

In attempting to answer the question, What's historical about Jesus?, I agreed with the scholarly conclusion that the Gospels' way of arranging the story of Jesus is not a reliable guide to the sequence of events, because the evangelists were interested less in historical reconstruction than in religious instruction.

The really critical issue is this: are the pattern and meaning that the Gospels give to Jesus due simply to the artistry of one writer whom everyone else copied? Or, as I will argue here, is a pattern that was embedded in the earliest Christian experience and memory faithfully mirrored in the Gospel narratives? If the fundamental identity of Jesus inscribed in the four canonical Gospels is that of a Messiah whose radical obedience to God is spelled out in self-emptying love for others, then the question is whether the pattern is imposed (for example, by Mark) at a relatively late date on recalcitrant materials, or whether it accurately conveys the understanding of Jesus by his earliest followers after the resurrection. Does it correspond, in other words, to the experience of "the real Jesus" in the Church?

I am calling this section "The Gospel and the Gospels" because I am trying to reverse the tendency of recent scholars to chop up the Gospels into separate sources that can be moved around at will, and the tendency to keep the Gospels isolated from all the other canonical writings. I am suggesting that if we look at the Gospels as literary compositions, quite a different conclusion emerges concerning the identity of Jesus. We then find as well that there is a profound unity of understanding concerning Jesus throughout the New Testament literature. The fundamental perception of Jesus in the canonical Gospels faithfully represents the identity of Jesus as it is expressed in our other earliest Christian writings.

We can begin by identifying the pattern that I suggest is central to all four canonical Gospels. Then we can see whether this "Gospel pattern" corresponds with the "pattern of the gospel" in our other earliest Christian sources. This is a very different way of thinking about "the historical Jesus," for it does not inquire into the facts of Jesus' existence, but the *meaning* of that existence as it shaped the "history" of Jesus' followers. It is an inquiry into the *historic* Jesus. At issue is the integrity and consistency of the interpretation of Christian identity rooted in Jesus the Lord.

We can begin with Mark's Gospel, as in all likelihood the first written. It is obvious that Mark uses a variety of traditions concerning Jesus. He uses many exorcism and healing stories, for example. Now, let us suppose that Mark's Gospel contained *only* such materials; his image of Jesus would then clearly be that of a wonder-worker. Mark also contains some wisdom traditions concerning Jesus, though not as many as Matthew and Luke: Jesus speaks in aphorisms, tells parables, discourses on the future. If Mark had chosen to gather *only* these materials into his account, then his image of Jesus would be that of the sage. But those choices are only hypothetical, because every careful reader of Mark knows that wisdom and wonder-working traditions in his Gospel have been subsumed by an image of Jesus that is far more pervasive: Jesus in Mark is the suffering Son of man.

The image is most obviously shaped by the passion account. In Mark, the passion of Jesus is even more dominant because of the brevity of his narrative as a whole. The suffering of Jesus is the climax to the story. The scandal of Jesus' death is not denied: he is fearful before his suffering, fails to defend himself before his accusers, is mocked and scourged, is betrayed by one disciple, denied by another, and abandoned by them all. He dies in apparent desolation. Yet Mark's telling of the story interprets these events not as the death of a sinner cursed by God, but as a "son of God" who knew his fate, accepted it, and understood it in the light of Scripture. Jesus is portrayed as one who dies in the most radical obedience to God: he declares, "Not what I will but what you will" (Mark 14:36). And his death is as well the most radical sort of service to humanity: "This is my blood of the covenant which is poured out for many" (Mark 14:24).

The image of Jesus as the one who suffers in obedience and in service is not found simply in the passion account. It dominates the earlier part of Mark's Gospel as well. Already in 3:6, a plot to destroy Jesus is begun, and in 3:20 the reader learns that a close follower of Jesus will join in that plot. Above all, Mark anticipates the suffering of Jesus by means of three increasingly explicit predictions of his passion (8:31; 9:31; 10:33–34). Of equal significance, Mark follows each of these predictions by a misunderstanding of discipleship by Jesus' followers (8:32; 9:33–34; 10:35–37). Jesus then responds to each misunderstanding in a way that connects the character of discipleship to his own destiny: those who wish to follow him must take up their cross and give up their lives (8:35–37); they must be like children and servants of all (9:35; 10:43). In short, Mark asserts, a disciple must follow the path of the Messiah: "For the Son of man also came not to be served but to serve, and to give his life as a ransom for many" (10:45).

To summarize: Mark's narrative has a tight focus on the identity of Jesus and the character of discipleship. Although Jesus is clearly filled with power and wisdom, and although these are revealed in his powerful works and words, Mark deliberately shapes the image of Jesus according to a pattern of suffering in service to others, and shows that discipleship means following in that same pattern. This *meaning* of Jesus is given, not by any of the single pieces, or their historical probability, or the quantitative balance among them, but by the structuring of the narrative as such. The meaning is given by story.

The Gospels of Matthew and Luke develop the image of Jesus in a distinctive way. Yet each keeps this same fundamental image of Jesus as the suffering Son of man. Each retains the Markan passion account and develops it even further. Each maintains the threefold prediction of the passion. By this means, they place Jesus' ministry of teaching and wonder-working within the framework of rejection and suffering. Something more than respect for a source is at work here. Matthew and Luke feel free to alter virtually every other aspect of Mark, but this image of the suffering One they do not alter in the least. Luke and Matthew accept the Markan interpretation of Jesus as religiously true. Their expansions and elaborations confirm rather than suppress this aspect of Jesus' identity.

Thus, in the context of dispute with a developing rabbinic Judaism, Matthew greatly expands the amount of material that demonstrates Jesus' role as a teacher, and in particular shows how Jesus interprets, fulfills, and even personifies Torah. In line with this portrayal of Jesus as "messianic teacher of the Church," Matthew also emphasizes the intelligence and teachability of the disciples, who are, after all, to "teach all that I have commanded" to the nations (Matt. 28:29). But Matthew also intensifies the picture of Jesus as suffering servant: he adds specific quotations from Torah that identify Jesus as the Isaian servant (Matt. 8:17; 12:18–21); he shows the internal dimension of Jesus' obedience as Son by including the account of the temptations (4:1–11); he heightens the drama of Jesus' rejection by the people to whom he was sent as proclaimer of the kingdom (27:25). Likewise, in his instructions on discipleship, Matthew not only agrees with Mark that the path of discipleship follows that of the suffering Messiah but deepens that understanding in terms of undergoing persecution from outsiders, and being a lowly servant to others within the community (5:11–12; 6:44; 10:16–24; 18:5–21; 24:9–14; 25:31–66).

The pattern of the suffering Messiah is, if anything, even more central to the plot of the two-volume work called Luke-Acts (the Gospel of Luke plus the Acts of the Apostles). Luke uses the scriptural pattern of the prophet like Moses (see Acts 7) to structure his story: Jesus is sent a first time to visit the people Israel for their salvation; out of ignorance they reject him; empowered by God in the resurrection, Jesus works again as prophet among the people through the apostles who speak and act "in his name." But they also experience as much rejection as acceptance. For Luke also, therefore, the heart both of the Scripture and of the good news is that "the Christ should suffer these things and enter into his glory" (Luke 24:26). In the narrative of Acts, Luke portrays the disciples-become-apostles in terms of their prophetic mission as workers of "signs and wonders among the people." For them also, however, the path of suffering marks the authentic following of the Messiah. Persecuted by the Sanhedrin, they leave "rejoicing that they were counted worthy to suffer dishonor for the name" (Acts 5:41); Paul is shown by the risen Lord "how much he must suffer for the sake of my name" (Acts 9:16); and Paul tells his young churches that "through many tribulations we must enter the kingdom of God" (Acts 14:22).

The Gospel of John is the real test case. The pattern in all three Synoptics, after all, could be attributed to their literary interdependence, even though Matthew and Luke each expand on Mark's emphasis on suffering in distinctive ways. In the Fourth Gospel, however, we are clearly outside the realm of literary dependence. The author of John probably shared some traditions with the Synoptics, but there is little or no reason to think he had knowledge of, or used, the synoptic Gospels as such. If the same pattern concerning the identity of Jesus and the character of discipleship is found also in John, its presence has considerable significance.

It would also be something of a surprise, given the distinctive way in which the Fourth Gospel has otherwise shaped the ministry of Jesus. I cataloged many of these differences from the Synoptics in chapter 5. The differences come to a focus in John's image of Jesus. In this Gospel, Jesus is above all the revealer of God (John 1:18), and reveals God by manifesting in creation and in human history the "glory" of God so fully and completely that in Jesus "the Word became flesh and dwelt among us" (John 1:14).

Ernst Käsemann once called John's portrayal of Jesus a "naive docetism." He meant that no matter how much Jesus is declared to be human in this Gospel, he does not really appear to be human. Jesus seems as much unearthly as earthly, even more "the man from heaven" than the "son of Joseph." This side of things can be overemphasized. For one thing, the Jesus of Mark's Gospel is scarcely a normal Jewish teacher either! The Jesus in John's Gospel is in some ways even more human than in the Synoptics. He experiences fatigue (4:6) and indecision (7:1–10) and anguish (12:7; 13:21). He is convulsed at the death of his friend Lazarus (11:33–35). He performs a miracle for the pleasure of it (2:1–11) and shows irritation (2:4; 6:26; 7:6–8; 8:25) and suspicion (2:24–25). He asks for a positive response from others (6:66–71). Only in this Gospel is Jesus portrayed as having friends (11:1–12:9). He has a disciple he prefers more than others (13:23; 19:26; 20:2; 21:20), asks Simon three times, "Do you love me more than these?" (21:15–17), and calls his followers "friends" (15:13–15).

Still, John's Gospel *does* emphasize Jesus' "otherness" in remarkable fashion: he "speaks as no man has ever spoken" (7:46). This portrayal is in large measure a function of the role Jesus has to play in John's Gospel. This Gospel encapsulates the whole drama of God's relationship with humanity, and Jesus is the central character. Jesus must therefore "represent" the Father to humanity, and the weight of that representative role necessarily demands of Jesus that he reveal more of "the Word" than of "the flesh."

The critical question is how John connects "glory" (the term associated with the revelation of God) to Jesus. Apart from the programmatic statement of the prologue ("we have seen his glory, glory as of the only begotten of God," 1:14), glory is attributed to a deed of Jesus only in 2:11. Otherwise, the "glory" that Jesus seeks is that of the Father who sent him (7:18; 8:50, 54; 9:24; 11:4, 40; 12:28, 43; 13:31). In this Gospel, Jesus is the obedient Son who speaks what his Father tells him (8:26–28) and works as he sees the Father working (5:19).

For this Gospel, furthermore, the supreme "work of God" that Jesus accomplishes is his passion and death. John identifies Jesus' passage back to God through his death and resurrection as his "glorification," and as the supreme revelation of God's "glory," that is, the effective presence of God in the world (see 7:39; 12:16, 23, 28; 13:31; 17:5).

The passion account is no more an afterthought for the Fourth Gospel than for the Synoptics. It is the climax that shapes the character of everything that precedes it. And Jesus is here also the suffering servant who in obedience to God gives his life for his fellow human beings. From the outside, Jesus is the victim of a plot made against him by Jewish opponents (5:18; 6:64; 7:1; 8:25). But for insiders, the death of Jesus is understood as a willing sacrifice for the sake of others, a death, as the high priest unwittingly prophesies, "for the nation, and not for the nation only, but to gather into one the children of God who are scattered abroad" (11:51–52). Thus, Jesus is the good shepherd who willingly lays down his life for the sheep (10:11, 15): "No one takes it from me, but I lay it down of my own accord" (10:18). Speaking of his death, he says, "Truly, truly I say to you, unless a grain of wheat falls into the earth and dies, it remains alone; but if it dies it bears much fruit" (12:24). And again, "Greater love has no man than this, that a man lay down his life for his friends" (15:13). It is from the side of the one who in his death cries, "I thirst" (19:28), that water flows (19:33), water that the reader knows is a symbol of the Spirit that is being handed over by Jesus (19:30) "which those who believed in him were to receive" (7:39).

Just as in the Synoptics, the pattern of Christ is to be the pattern of Christian discipleship. They will be hated by the world that hated Jesus (15:18–21), and they will experience tribulation (16:33). They must be willing to give up their lives for others as well: "He who loves his life loses it, and he who hates his life in this world will keep it for eternal life. If anyone serves me, he must follow me" (12:25–26). As Jesus has loved his disciples, so he orders them to love one another (13:54; 15:12). As Jesus has shown himself a servant in their midst by washing their feet, so should they with one another: "I have left you an example, that you also should do what I have done to you" (13:17). And the Gospel's epilogue predicts Peter's death in terms that echo Jesus' own: "This he said to show by what death he was to glorify God. And after this he said 'Follow me'" (21:19).

To summarize: the four canonical Gospels are remarkably consistent on one essential aspect of the identity and mission of Jesus. Their fundamental focus is not on Jesus' wondrous deeds nor on his wise words. Their shared focus is on the *character* of his life and death. They all reveal the same *pattern* of radical obedience to God and selfless love toward other people. All four Gospels also agree that discipleship is to follow the same *messianic pattern*. They do not emphasize the performance of certain deeds or the learning of certain doctrines. They insist on living according to the same pattern of life and death shown by Jesus.

This interpretation of Jesus and of discipleship in all four Gospels is given by the shape of the narratives themselves, by connections established within and by means of the story. When the story told by these narratives is dismantled, their interpretation also disappears.

The Truth That Is in Jesus

If we look at the other New Testament writings, do we find the same pattern of messiahship and discipleship, connected in the same way? In Paul, as we have seen, there is no full narrative about Jesus, even though Paul makes a number of discrete references to Jesus' earthly life. But Paul does *refer* to the story of Jesus. With some frequency, he alludes to, or applies to situations, a basic story pattern concerning Jesus. And it is clear that when he does so, he expects such allusions and applications to be understood by his readers. The implication? Paul can assume among his readers a shared knowledge of this basic "story pattern" about Jesus.

One of the more obvious and striking examples is found in Galatians 2:20, where Paul declares: "I have been crucified with Christ; it is no longer I who live, but Christ who lives in me; and the life I now live in the flesh I live by the faith of the son of God who loved me and gave himself for me." We are naturally struck by the assertion that "Christ lives" in Paul; this picks up what I was describing earlier as the "resurrection experience." The "real Jesus" for Paul is the one who lives within the community. But even more startling is the way Paul connects this experience of Jesus' continuing (more powerful) life with the story of his crucifixion, *which is also at work in his disciple Paul!* And then, Paul spells out the inner meaning of the crucifixion: the death of Jesus is an expression of Jesus' faith in God and Jesus' love for humanity. Please note that this is precisely the "messianic pattern" that I have described in the four Gospels.

Galatians 2:20 therefore shows us a tiny piece of narrative concerning Jesus that Paul regards as powerful and normative for himself and his readers. *Paul* has been crucified; *he* lives by the gift of Jesus' faith and Jesus' love toward *him*. That Paul understands this mystical connectedness to the power of Jesus' story to be real, not only for himself but also for his readers, is indicated in the following verses, where he speaks of "Christ publicly displayed as crucified" before them and their "hearing by faith," and of God supplying "the Spirit to you and [working] miracles among you" (Gal. 3:1–5). Similarly, Paul states later in the same letter, "If we live by the Spirit, let us also walk by the Spirit" (5:25). What behavior does he think meets that norm? "Bear one another's burdens and so fulfill the Law of Christ" (6:2). The way Paul uses the term *nomos Christou* ("law of Christ") here is clearly equivalent to what I have been calling the "messianic pattern": in the community of faith, the work of the Holy Spirit is to replicate among believers the pattern of selfless service that Jesus demonstrated by his death.

In 1 Corinthians, Paul speaks of the *nous Christou* ("the mind of Christ") as an understanding that is measured, not by the "wisdom of the world," but specifically by the "wisdom of the cross." He means by this a sense of how the gifts of the Spirit are to be used appropriately for the building up of the community (see 1 Cor. 1:18–2:16). Paul's discussion in 1 Corinthians 8–10 of whether Christians could eat food that had been offered to idols shows how this "mind of Christ" is applied to practical circumstances. In 8:11, Paul states the key principle of edification: a legitimate right is relativized by the needs of a brother or sister—"And so by your knowledge this weak man is destroyed, the brother for whom Christ died. Thus, sinning against your brethren and wounding their conscience when it is weak, you sin against Christ." In this passage there is none of the intense personal "mysticism" that some have detected in Galatians 2:20–21. But Paul assumes just as real a connection between the story of Jesus and the behavior of the community. Notice the force of the short allusion, "the brother for whom Christ died," which is the same sort of narrative fragment as in Galatians 2:20. The death of Jesus for the members of the community establishes a real connection between him and them: when a brother's faith is destroyed, "you sin against Christ" (1 Cor. 8:12).

The pattern of Jesus' death for others is again cited as normative for community behavior in 1 Corinthians 11:17–32. Paul rebukes the Corinthians for their abuses of the common meal: "Do you despise the church of God and humiliate those who have nothing?" In response to their behavior, Paul refers to the words of Jesus "on the night when he was betrayed." Paul had received this tradition, he says, "from the Lord" (11:23). After quoting the words of Jesus over the bread and wine—the bread is his body "which is for you" (11:24), and the wine is his blood "of the new covenant" (11:25)—Paul applies this part of Jesus' story to his community's behavior: "Whoever, therefore, eats the bread or drinks the cup of the Lord in an unworthy manner will be guilty of profaning the body and blood of the Lord" (11:27). But what does Paul mean by an "unworthy manner"? It is eating and drinking "without discerning the body" (11:29). By this compact expression, Paul manages to draw together the symbols of the community meal and the ideal self-image of the community itself: they are to be shaped by the meal-memory of One who "gave his body" for others, into a manner of life that "builds up the body" of the community (see 12:12, 27).

Paul again uses the Jesus story—not the facts of his life but the meaning of his life—as the basis for community instruction in the Letter to the Romans. Remember that this is a community that Paul has never met. Its members have not previously been instructed by him. If he uses elements from the Jesus story, and expects them to grasp his point, he must be able to assume that these early Christians also were aware both of the story and of its essential character.

In Romans 13:14, Paul tells his Roman readers to "put on the Lord Jesus" and not gratify their selfish desires. This tight connection between identification with Jesus (putting on Jesus) and a life of selflessness (not gratifying selfish desires) is spelled out in Paul's discussion of the readers' disputes over diet and other practical observances. He insists that the norm for their behavior should be the building up of one another's faith: "If your brother is being injured by what you eat, you are no longer walking in love. Do not let what you eat cause the ruin of one for whom Christ died" (14:15).

Notice that "the one for whom Christ died" is the same kind of compressed bit of story that we saw Paul using in 1 Corinthians 8:11, "the brother for whom Christ died." In both cases, the death of Jesus is understood as an act of love for others that is paradigmatic for the attitudes and actions of Jesus' followers within the community, and that is the measure of their own love ("you are no longer walking in love").

Paul applies the pattern of the Jesus story twice more in the same section of Romans. The strong are to bear with the weak and should not seek to please themselves. Why? "For Christ did not please himself; but, as it is written, 'the reproaches of those who reproached thee fell on me'" (Rom. 15:1–3; see LXX Ps. 68:10). The use of a psalm that otherwise plays such an important role in interpreting the death of Jesus (compare John 15:25; 19:28; Mark 15:23, 36; Matt. 27:34, 48; Luke 23:36; Acts 1:20) is itself significant. It shows how such interpretation was taking place in Pauline as well as in synoptic circles. But more striking is the simple use of "for" to establish a warrant: they are not to please themselves *for* (that is, "because") Christ did not please himself, but served others. Finally, Paul invokes the entire pattern of Jesus' work as Messiah when he exhorts the Roman Christians, "Welcome one another, then, as Christ has welcomed you, for the glory of God" (15:7).

The clearest example of how Paul applies the pattern of the Jesus story as the measure of Christian behavior is found in his letter to the Philippians. In Philippians 2:1–11, Paul exhorts his readers to have unity among themselves. He appeals to the work of the Spirit in the community, which should lead them to share a single outlook. He then spells this out in terms of an attitude that does not seek private benefit but rather the good of others (2:1–4). Remarkably, Paul explicitly joins this attitude to that held by Jesus. As the Revised Standard Version translates the Greek, "Have this mind among yourselves which is yours in Christ Jesus" (Phil. 2:5). The sense of the passage is that these Christians should have the same outlook and behavior as Jesus.

Paul then provides the illustration of this "way of thinking" by explicit reference to the way Jesus "regarded" himself and the way he acted with respect to his own benefit. The passage is intensely poetic. Some scholars think it was an earlier Christian hymn that Paul is here quoting. If that is the case, then this understanding, to make the point one more time, goes back to at most a few years after the death of Jesus. Whether it is a hymn he is using, or his own composition, the passage perfectly illustrates his point:

> Who, though he was in the form of God,
>
> did not count equality with God a thing to be grasped, but
>
> emptied himself, taking the form
>
> of a servant, being born
>
> in the human likeness.
>
> And being found in human form,
>
> he humbled himself and became obedient unto death,
>
> even death on a cross.

Some scholars argue that the passage describes the incarnation of a preexistent one. But with other scholars, I hold that the entire passage describes the "messianic outlook" of Jesus in his human life. In either case, from "being found in human form, he humbled himself and became obedient unto death, even death on a cross" (2:8), the reference to the earthly Jesus is clear. In this case, the "way Jesus thought" is explicitly recommended to the Philippians as the measure of how they should "think" in community: they are to follow the pattern of a Messiah whose servantlike obedience to God is the paradigm for mutual service within the community (2:1–4).

A pause for summation: in four of Paul's undisputed letters, he makes explicit use of the Jesus story in his moral exhortation to communities. He does not employ *facts* from the Jesus tradition, but rather the *pattern* of obedient service and selfless love, as a paradigm for attitudes and actions among his readers.

Three quick corollaries: first, Paul obviously *was* interested in the "story of Jesus" as normative for how Christians should live (that is, discipleship). Second, the pattern he enunciates is *exactly* the same as that given by all four canonical Gospels, and among all the gospels, only by them. Third, the use of this pattern by Paul decades before the composition of the Gospels (and his assumption that this pattern is already known to readers he himself did not convert) supports the position that this pattern was not a late invention but rather an early memory, perhaps the earliest of formative memories, concerning "the real Jesus."

Suppose someone raises this objection: only the so-called Pauline Christianity invented this understanding of the Jesus story, and through its influence imposed it on other, equally normative memories, with the obvious channel being Mark's Gospel. The objection would have to account for two critical pieces of evidence. First, Paul claims to preach the same gospel as the Palestinian witnesses to the resurrection, and he repeatedly assumes that the traditions concerning Jesus were a common possession of the community. But if this is simply Pauline special pleading? The second piece of evidence is the presence of the same pattern in the Gospel of John, which cannot be said to depend on Pauline Christianity, and which is also (in the view of the majority of scholars) not dependent on the synoptic tradition.

There is, however, still further evidence for the pattern I have been describing. We can find it, for example, in the Letter to the Ephesians. I think that this letter was written by Paul. The majority of scholars consider it pseudonymous. In either case, Ephesians uses the Jesus story as paradigm for Christian discipleship. In 4:17–19, for example, the author warns his readers not to live in the way of the Gentiles. He concludes: "You did not so learn Christ—assuming that you have heard about him and were taught in him *as the truth is in Jesus*" (4:20–21; emphasis added). The use of the personal name *Jesus* is very striking. So is the suggestion that the "way" (*kathōs*) to learn the pattern of the Messiah is according to the truth that is "in Jesus." The application of the pattern is made explicit in 4:32: ". . . be kind to one another, tenderhearted, forgiving one another, as God in Christ forgave you." This might seem at first to be simply a theological proposition, but 5:2 shows the author to be alluding to a story: ". . . and walk in love as Christ loved us and gave himself up for us, a fragrant offering and sacrifice to God." The phrase *loved us and gave himself up for us* is a narrative fragment. It is very close to Galatians 2:20, which we looked at previously. Ephesians understands Jesus' obedient self-sacrifice to be an act of love for others, and says that this should be the pattern for relations within the community.

I earlier pointed out how many allusions to the facts of Jesus' ministry there are in the Letter to the Hebrews: his being Jewish (2:15), of the tribe of Judah (7:14), tested (2:18); his praying for deliverance from death (5:7); and his being crucified (12:2) outside the city (13:12). The argument of Hebrews, however, focuses on the death and resurrection of Jesus as a royal enthronement and as a priestly act that enables access to God. Critical to this argument is that the priesthood of Jesus is rooted in his humanity and involves not simply his body but the free disposition of himself in obedience to God. Thus, in contrast to the priests of the earlier covenant who offered the blood of goats, Jesus "offered up himself" (7:27). In a remarkable bit of rhetoric, Hebrews places LXX Psalm 39 on the lips of Jesus: "When he came into the world, he said, 'sacrifices and offerings thou hast not desired, but a body thou hast prepared for me . . . then I said, "Lo, I have come to do thy will O God". . . ' " (Heb. 10:5–7), and draws the conclusion, "by that will we have been sanctified through the offering of the body of Jesus Christ once for all" (Heb. 10:10).

For Hebrews, Jesus' suffering was the path toward becoming fully Son of God and perfect priest: "although he was a son, he learned obedience through what he suffered; and being made perfect, he became the source of eternal salvation to all who obey him" (5:9). This "messianic pattern," in turn, is the paradigm for their own discipleship. As the author exhorts the readers to endure their suffering as a form of instruction as children of God ("you are enduring for the sake of an education," 12:7), he tells them to "look to Jesus, the pioneer and perfecter of faith, who for the joy that was set before him endured the cross, despising the shame, and is seated at the right hand of the throne of God" (12:2). Even more directly, Hebrews moves from this observation, "So Jesus also suffered outside the camp in order to sanctify the people through his own blood" (13:12), to this immediate application, "Therefore let us go forth to him outside the camp and bear the abuse he endured" (13:13). The pattern of the Messiah and the pattern of discipleship are linked: each must pass through the suffering that is intrinsic to obedience.

There is no real reason why the composition known as 1 Peter could not have been written by Peter the apostle. Most scholars, however, consider it to have been written near the end of the first century. What is important to the present argument is that this letter uses the story of Jesus to exhort its readers. Once more, it is not the facts of Jesus' ministry that are cited as important but the basic pattern of his death and resurrection. Thus, in speaking of the prophets, the author says, "They inquired what person or time was indicated by the Spirit of Christ within them when predicting the sufferings of Christ and the subsequent glory" (1 Pet. 1:10–11). Farther on, the readers are told that they "have been ransomed . . . by the precious blood of Christ" (1:19). Most impressively, they are told to endure patiently when they suffer for doing right: "For to this you have been called, because Christ also suffered for you, leaving an example that you should follow in his steps" (2:21). We see here the same connections that have been made by Paul, Hebrews, and the Gospels: the fundamental *call* of discipleship involves suffering, for the call is based on following the pattern of the Messiah, "who suffered for" them.

What is more remarkable is that the author then spells out this example in terms of the *manner* of Jesus' suffering: "He committed no sin; no guile was found on his lips. When he was reviled, he did not revile in return; when he suffered, he did not threaten; but he trusted to him who judges justly" (2:23). This passage is cast in the form of a story. It is obviously influenced by the suffering servant account in Isaiah 53:4–9 (see also Acts 8:32–33). But it is also obviously *not* derived literarily from any of the Gospel accounts. The author then makes explicit the connection between what Jesus did and the story now being lived by the readers: "He himself bore our sins in his body on the tree, that we might die to sin and live to righteousness. By his wounds you have been healed. For you were straying like sheep, but have now returned to the shepherd and guardian of your souls" (1 Pet. 2:24–25). As in the case of Romans 15:1–3, this passage shows us how the basic *pattern* of the Jesus story was interpreted in the light of Scripture and applied as a paradigm to the life of discipleship, which is understood precisely as a "following in the steps" of Jesus, through present suffering to future glory with God.

Conclusions

By looking at the "story of Jesus" not in terms of a collection of facts or in terms of a pile of discrete pieces, but in terms of *pattern* and *meaning*, we have found a deep consistency in the earliest Christian literature concerning the character of Jesus as Messiah.

The conviction sometimes takes the form of a narrative epitome, an abbreviated form of the "story of Jesus" that is applied to the lives of believers. It expresses the meaning of Jesus' ministry in terms of its ending: Jesus is the suffering servant whose death is a radical act of obedience toward God and an expression of loving care for his followers.

Both in the Gospels and in the epistolary literature, this "messianic pattern" is explicitly connected to an understanding of discipleship. To be a member of the messianic community is to live according to this "mind of Christ," to express obedient faith in God by loving service to the neighbor.

When the witness of the New Testament is taken as a whole, a deep consistency can be detected beneath its surface diversity. The "real Jesus" is first of all the powerful, resurrected Lord whose transforming Spirit is active in the community. But following Jesus is not a matter of the sort of power that dominates others, nor of "already ruling" in the kingdom of God (1 Cor. 4:8). It is instead a matter of transformation according to the pattern of the Messiah. The "real Jesus" is therefore also the one who through the Spirit replicates in the lives of believers faithful obedience to God and loving service to others. Everywhere in these writings the image of Jesus involves the tension-filled paradox of death and resurrection, suffering and glory.

Within the New Testament, no other pattern joins the story of Jesus and that of his followers. Discipleship does not consist in a countercultural critique of society. Discipleship does not consist in working overwhelming miracles. These elements of the Jesus tradition are not made normative in the way that the pattern of obedient suffering and loving service is.

In short, abandoning the frame of meaning given to the story of Jesus by the four canonical Gospels is to abandon the frame of meaning given to the story of Jesus and of Christian discipleship by the rest of the New Testament as well.

In the light of these simple observations, the question must be asked, Is what is claimed to be a pursuit of the historical Jesus not in truth a kind of flight from the image of Jesus and of discipleship inexorably ingrained in these texts? For our present age, in which the "wisdom of the world" is expressed in individualism, narcissism, preoccupation with private rights, and competition, the "wisdom of the cross" is the most profoundly countercultural message of all. Instead of an effort to rectify the distorting effect of the Gospel narratives, the effort to reconstruct Jesus according to some other pattern appears increasingly as an attempt to flee the scandal of the gospel.

Critical Scholarship and the Church

In this book, I have tried to bring some clarity to a conceptually and culturally confused discussion concerning the historical Jesus and the implications of Historical Jesus research for Christian faith. Here are some of the major points I have tried to establish:

1. History is a limited mode of human knowing. Historical analysis can yield real knowledge about earliest Christianity and the figure of Jesus. But there are intractable limits to this knowledge. When inquiry seeks to surmount those limits, evidence is distorted and history itself is discredited.

2. The New Testament writings yield some historical information, but that is not what they do best. And when the compositions are fragmented, chopped into small pieces, and arranged in arbitrary sequences, they do not work at all. The literary compositions of the New Testament are analyzed best when their literary integrity is respected and appreciated. Approached in this fashion, they can be appreciated as witnesses and interpretations of religious experiences and convictions.

3. Despite the obvious diversity in genre, perspective, and theme in the New Testament compositions, the coherence of their generative experiences and convictions can be glimpsed from their remarkable consistency concerning the image of Jesus and of discipleship.

4. If the expression *the real Jesus* is used at all, it should not refer to a historically reconstructed Jesus. Such a Jesus is not "real" in any sense, except as a product of scholarly imagination. The Christians' claim to experience the "real Jesus" in the present, on the basis of religious experiences and convictions, can be challenged on a number of fronts (religious, theological, moral), but not historically.

5. Corresponding to the Christian claim, there is a "real Jesus" in the texts of the New Testament as they have been transmitted to this generation. It is a Jesus inscribed literarily in the New Testament compositions *as* compositions. Jesus appears there as a definite, indeed unmistakably specific person, who defines by his life and death a pattern of existence measured in terms of obedience and suffering, service and love.

One further aspect of the cultural confusion remains to be discussed. I hope that the shape of this book makes it evident that I think about these things both as a Christian and as a critical scholar. My final remarks touch on the possibilities for a truly critical biblical scholarship within a church that is also faithful to its Lord.

The Credibility of Christianity

From the start, Christianity has been rooted in the paradoxical claim that a human being executed as a criminal is the source of God's life-giving and transforming Spirit. From the start, this "good news" has been regarded as foolishness to the wise of the world. Christianity has never been able to "prove" its claims except by appeal to the experiences and convictions of those already convinced. The only real validation for the claim that Christ is what the creed claims him to be, that is, light from light, true God from true God, is to be found in the quality of life demonstrated by those who make this confession.

Only if Christians and Christian communities illustrate lives transformed according to the pattern of faithful obedience and loving service found in Jesus does their claim to live by the Spirit of Jesus have any validity. The claims of the gospel cannot be demonstrated logically. They cannot be proved historically. They can be validated only existentially by the witness of authentic Christian discipleship.

The more the church has sought to ground itself in something other than the transforming work of the Spirit, the more it has sought to buttress its claims by philosophy or history, the more it has sought to defend itself against its cultured despisers by means of sophisticated apology, the more also it has missed the point of its existence, which is not to take a place within worldly wisdom but to bear witness to the reality of a God who transforms suffering and death with the power of new life.

Christianity has credibility, both with its own adherents and with its despisers, to the degree that it claims and lives by its own distinctive identity. This means, at a minimum, recognizing that Christianity is not measured by cultural expectations but by the experiences and convictions by which it lives. A church that has lost a sense of its boundaries—that is, a grasp of its self-definition—can only recover it by reasserting its character as a community of faith with a canon of Scripture and a creed.

The erosion of these boundaries has been exposed in the current Historical Jesus debate. There has been no clear sense of where "the church" stands as a community concerning the historical Jesus. Indeed, as we have seen, official leaders of a church, like Bishop Spong, have expressed opinions that are, on the face of it, incompatible with the classical Christian creed. "Christians" have been strung all along the continuum of stimulus and response in this discussion. But there is no explicit realm of discourse that can be called the church's.

One reason has been the loss within the church of any sense of how the Scripture can function as a basis for debate and decision making in response to crisis. This loss, in turn, is in considerable measure owing to the hegemony of the historical critical method. Several generations of scholars and theologians have been disabled from direct and responsible engagement with the texts of the tradition in their religious dimension. Even more obvious has been the disappearance of the creed as a meaningful framework for reading Scripture and undertaking theological discourse within the Christian community.

It is not at all obvious *how* Christians can recover some sense of community, canon, and creed. The present polarization and distrust between conservative and liberal tendencies within Christianity make the recovery more difficult. But a start might be the simple recognition that whatever the church's discourse is, it should not be the same as the academy's, nor should it be subject to the same rules or the same criteria of validity. It is time for a return from the academic captivity of the church. It is time for Christians to recognize that not every intellectual tendency or shift of mood is one that enhances the church's fundamental responsibility for handing on a tradition of life from one generation to another.

The place where this modest change of heart must take place is where the double-mindedness is most obvious, namely, in seminaries, divinity schools, and schools of theology. If the church is to be renewed as a community of faith with a distinctive, functional, and flexible mode of discourse, if it is to live by a canon of Scripture and within the rule of faith, then professors within Christian seminaries need to find a way to combine a commitment to tradition with intellectual integrity and freedom. But at the very least, such professors should be willing to make their fundamental commitment to the tradition, and not simply to the ever-shifting sands of scholarly fashion.

Allow me to speak as just such a teacher of New Testament in a seminary. Shouldn't we communicate to students that the church is not really only an institutionalized form of racism, sexism, homophobia, and speciesism, but is a place in the world where the power of resurrection life can be realized and enacted? Shouldn't we treat the canon of Scripture as something more than the arbitrary or ideologically motivated preemptive suppression of variety in the ancient church by patriarchal bishops, and show students how the fundamental issue of the character of God's gift in the crucified Messiah, and therefore also the character of discipleship in response to that gift, was and is at stake in the question of which documents are to be read in the church? Shouldn't we be willing to assert with students, as every Christian theologian before us was willing to assert, that Jesus is Son of God made flesh, before raising the question of how that paradoxical statement can be intellectually engaged?

Most of all, we need to understand the primary task of theology not to be the reform of the world's social structures, nor the ideological critique of the church as institution, nor the discovery of what is false or distorting in religious behavior, but the discernment and articulation of the work of the living God. Within the Christian community, this means the discernment of the ways in which the transformative power of the Spirit of the risen Christ is present and active, as well as the ways it is resisted and impeded. It means articulating the implications of God's work in human experience for the response of the church in obedience and service. By such theological activity, the story of Jesus comes alive both within the texts of human experience and in the texts of the New Testament.

Those of us who are entrusted with the formation of Christianity's ministers and leaders ought, I think, to take less seriously the judgment of our academic colleagues and more seriously the judgment of God, "before whose judgment seat we all shall stand" (Rom. 14:10). We need to ask not only what we are teaching but also what we are failing to teach. We can begin by affirming what is positive in the gift of God in Jesus Christ and what is of astonishing and transformative power in the story of Jesus, before asking what is lacking in it and how it might need supplementing from other traditions. We should, in a word, ask of one another, before and during our criticism of the Christian tradition, an explicit and exquisite loyalty to it.

The Role of Critical Biblical Scholarship

If such loyalty is to be an authentic expression of faith, however, it must also *be* critical. Ultimate human loyalty is appropriately directed to the living God rather than to community memory. The task of theology in the church is not only discernment of God's word and praise of God's work, but also critical reflection on the received tradition and the adequacy of the human response to God.

Biblical scholarship can play a key role in such critical reflection. It has failed to play that role adequately because it has for too long attached itself to a narrow construal of "critical." In biblical scholarship, "critical" has tended to be identified with "historical." The historical critical method, furthermore, has tended to be overly critical of the tradition and insufficiently critical of itself. For biblical scholarship to play its appropriate critical role within Christian theology—and my argument here concerns *only* its function within the church as distinct from the academy—it requires a broader and more comprehensive model for the apprehension of the New Testament writings as such, and requires as well a more inclusive sense of "criticism."

A MORE COMPREHENSIVE MODEL

One of the remarkable features of the academy is that scholars, who analyze everything else with such ease, so seldom and so poorly analyze their own procedures. That is not entirely true, of course, for scholars are always criticizing each other's use of methods. But the attention usually falls precisely on method: was a certain procedure carried out correctly, or were the criteria properly applied? What is often lacking is reflection on the fundamental models or paradigms within which methods function. These are often what is "taken for granted" or "assumed." They are also what are often most in need of criticism.

The use of the historical critical method in biblical scholarship is an obvious example. The very phrase is misleading, for historians use a variety of methods and procedures. What is conventionally called a "method" is, in reality, a *model*. I use the term *model* to mean an imaginative construal of the subject being studied, as well as a structured picture of both process and product: a model is a paradigm within which the data pertinent to a discipline makes sense.

In answer to the question, What are the New Testament writings about?, the historical model responds that they are about the history of early Christianity, including its founder. The goal of inquiry is the description, and possibly even the reconstruction, of historical development. For this goal, the writings of the New Testament have importance as *sources* for such a reconstruction. Ideally, if the goal of a satisfactory reconstruction were achieved, the sources would not need to be revisited. The historical model provides no compelling reason for reading the New Testament except to correct or improve the historical account of earliest Christianity.

I hope I have made clear that I see nothing problematic about the historical model in itself. It is obviously important to study Christian origins historically. And in such historical inquiry, faith commitments should play no role. Christianity is no more privileged for the historian than any other human phenomenon. My reservations have to do with the difficulties this model has in reaching its goal in this case: the writings of the New Testament are too few, too fragmentary, and too lacking in chronological and geographical controls to enable a truly comprehensive reconstruction of Christian origins.

The greater problem with the historical critical model is that until very recently it has tended to dominate scholarship to the exclusion of other approaches. As a result, the historical critical model comes to be equated simply with "critical." But by reducing everything to a single dimension, the historical model distorts what it can know and misses a great deal of what is important to know.

New Testament scholars need a model that enables them to approach the texts in as many ways as the texts approach us. At least four dimensions of the New Testament texts should be taken into account.

1. Anthropological: These writings are thoroughly human in the process of their composition. Appeals to divine inspiration are claims about the ultimate origin of the texts and their authority. Inspiration is not a key to the interpretation of the texts. The anthropological dimension also considers that

the texts result from real human persons interpreting their experience, and seeking to understand their experience with available cultural symbols. It recognizes that religious literature is generated by real experiences and convictions, and not simply by aesthetic concerns.

2. Historical: The writers of the New Testament were not Trobrianders. They were Jews of the first-century Mediterranean world. Their experiences and convictions, therefore, were necessarily interpreted within a symbolic framework specific to that place and time. The complex overlap of Mediterranean, Greco-Roman, and Jewish cultures affected the shaping of this literature. Above all, the experiences of the first Christians were clothed with the garments of Torah. If the anthropological dimension establishes connections between readers and these texts, the historical dimension demands coming to grips with the cultural "otherness" of the writings. Recognizing the historical dimension of the texts (as an essential aspect of their interpretation) is not the same as using the texts for historical reconstruction.

3. Literary: The canon of the New Testament consists of compositions that are diverse in their literary fashioning, perspectives, and purposes. The meaning of texts is inextricably connected with their literary construction. Gaining access to such meaning demands of the interpreter, therefore, a genuine engagement with the literary complexities of the respective compositions. As I have suggested, one of the great deficiencies of the historical critical model has been its disregard for this dimension, leading to the fragmentation of the texts into smaller pieces that can be used as historical sources. It is certainly true that some New Testament compositions were complex in their construction and did make use of earlier sources. But the final literary form of such texts was canonized, and only attention to this given literary dimension can accurately be called the interpretation of the "New Testament." It is striking that all the Historical Jesus research we have surveyed begins with the *elimination* of the literary structure of the Gospels.

4. Religious: These compositions were produced by members of a religious movement for other members of that movement. More than that, specifically religious experiences and convictions generated the compositions. To read these compositions in terms simply of the historical information they provide is to miss the most important and most explicit insight they offer the

reader, namely, how the experience of the powerful transforming power of God that came through the crucified Messiah Jesus created not only a new understanding of who Jesus was but, simultaneously, a new understanding of God and God's way with the world.

A more adequate model for reading the New Testament, then, can be called an "experience/interpretation" model. The model takes seriously the deeply human character of the writings, the experiences and convictions that generated them, and the cultural and historical symbols they appropriate. It enables the scholar to apprehend the historical dimensions of the New Testament texts without forcing them to perform a task for which they are ill-equipped, namely, to serve as sources for a reconstruction of Christian origins. More significantly, the model enables other crucial dimensions of the texts to be apprehended and appreciated as well. Best of all, it is a model that enables a community of faith that also experiences the powerful presence of the risen Lord to engage these texts (together with those of Torah) in a continuing conversation. The model for understanding how the New Testament compositions came into existence, in other words, also provides a framework for interpreting these compositions within the life of the church.

THE MEANING OF CRITICAL SCHOLARSHIP

New Testament scholarship within the church should be critical first of all by being self-critical. Because so much of the work done within the framework of the historical critical method lacked such self-examination, its hidden normative assumptions remained untested. The development of "ideological criticism" among contemporary scholars begins with the recognition that literature and art are not neutral but always have an interest. Some of this criticism has focused on the ideological interest of the New Testament writings (e.g., their patriarchalism) without also taking into account the ideological agenda of the interpreter.

The more recent tendency in scholarship to identify and name the ideological commitments of the interpreter is a positive step. Other critics can then evaluate fairly the extent to which such an ideological starting point enables readings and the extent to which it suppresses readings. They can also test the degree to which readings are consistent with declared perspectives.

Epilogue

It is entirely appropriate for an interpreter to declare an allegiance to the traditional Christian code as the ideological starting point for his or her interpretation. The readings generated by such an interpreter can then fairly be tested by reference to that code. It would be equally appropriate for those who detested and despised traditional Christianity and sought to destroy it by means of undermining confidence in its normative texts to state their commitment clearly, so that their efforts also could be fairly evaluated by their chosen standard. In recent Historical Jesus scholarship, such clear declarations of ideological starting points have mostly been lacking. The exceptions, like Stephen Mitchell, are to be appreciated for their candor.

Biblical scholarship can also be "critical" of the New Testament texts themselves in ways that the "historical critical" model did not allow. I have repeatedly challenged the premise that any historical reconstruction can, by itself, function as normative. Without a community's commitment to acknowledge "a more adequate history" as normative, the criticism of tradition carried out by historical research is strictly beside the point. In fact, however, Christian faith and Christian theology have never made such a commitment to the normativity of historical reconstruction. They have instead made a commitment to the "history" limned in the texts of the New Testament, and above all to the "story of Jesus" inscribed in the Gospel narratives.

But the texts of the New Testament are open to criticism on other than historical fronts. They can be challenged morally, religiously, and theologically for their adequacy, consistency, and cogency. Do the texts of the New Testament when taken at face value support a structure of society in which women are oppressed? Such texts can best be criticized, not by constructing an imaginary, alternative history of early Christianity in which women enjoyed equality, but on the basis of theological convictions that God's Spirit has brought to maturity within the church. Does the New Testament's inherited monotheism bring with it a virus of intolerance toward diversity that has infected Christian attitudes and behavior? These texts can best be criticized, not by inventing a history of Christianity that was non-Jewish, but by invoking other moral and religious principles within the texts to counter the virus of intolerance.

Within an ecclesial hermeneutics that begins with the premise that God's Spirit is working in the world to transform people into the image of the "real

Jesus," the discernment of the complex texts of human experience are brought into conversation with the complex and often conflicting voices of the normative texts of tradition. The diverse voices in the canon are allowed to converse with the diverse voices of contemporary experience. Contradictions in the scriptural texts can be exploited to provide new insights into the "mind of Christ" by which the church seeks to live. Biblical scholarship need not be "historical" in order to be "critical."

Finally, "critical" can mean allowing the texts to criticize the practices of the church and the assumptions of the tradition. This is obviously a legitimate and important function of scholarship within the church. It is what was originally intended by Luther's principle of *sola scriptura*. Luther recognized that without a dialectical relationship to the texts, in which they were given their own authority over the church, tradition could swallow them up and manipulate them to its own ends.

I have shown how the historical critical method inherited this perspective. A mistake was made, however, when the critical function was given to historical reconstruction rather than to the texts themselves. In truth, the sort of criticism of the church intended by Luther is located in the texts and not outside them. Here is where contemporary Historical Jesus research has most seriously missed the point. The Jesus Seminar, for example, declared its animosity toward a Jesus purveyed by televangelists. It regarded this Jesus as too much shaped in the direction of the divine by later doctrine. It saw this Jesus as too much the figure of eschatology.

But what the Seminar failed to understand was that these images—if they are, indeed, seen as negative—would best be criticized *from within* the Gospel narratives themselves, not by constructing an "alternative fiction," or an image of Jesus recoverable only by dismantling the texts. If the Jesus Seminar is concerned about Christianity's preoccupation with Armageddon, then there are more than sufficient texts within the canon of the New Testament to challenge that obsession. The attempt to create a "noneschatological Jesus" not only distorts history, it is bad tactics. Those who consider the end of the world to be the gist of Jesus' message are convinced that it is found in the texts. Only the demonstration that the texts themselves do not support such an overemphasis, and indeed combat such an emphasis, can be convincing.

In *The Five Gospels* the Jesus Seminar warns against looking for a comfortable Jesus. That is sound advice. What I have tried to demonstrate in this book, however, is that the truly uncomfortable Jesus, the genuinely "counter-cultural" Jesus, is not the one reconstructed according to the ethos of contemporary academics—whether it is Crossan's politically correct revolutionary Jesus or Borg's charismatic-founder Jesus or any of the others—but the one inscribed in the canonical Gospels. The Jesus who truly challenges this age, as every age, is the one who suffers in obedience to God and calls others to such suffering service in behalf of humanity. This is the Jesus that classical Christianity has always proclaimed; this is an understanding of discipleship to which classical Christianity has always held.

Does the church act triumphalistically, or treat its people arrogantly? Is it an agent for the suppression of human needs and aspirations? Does it foster intolerance and small-mindedness? Does the church proclaim a gospel of success and offer Jesus as a better business partner? Does it encourage an ethos of prosperity to the neglect of the earth's good, or an individualistic spirituality to the neglect of the world's needy? Are its leaders corrupt and coercive? Such distortions of Christianity can find no harsher critic, no more radical rejecter, than the Jesus found *only* in the pages of the New Testament, the Jesus who was himself emptied out for others and called his followers to do the same.

The Jesus to whom Saint Francis of Assisi appealed in his call for a poor and giving rather than a powerful and grasping church was not the Historical Jesus but the Jesus of the Gospels. One must only wonder why this Jesus is not also the "real Jesus" for those who declare a desire for religious truth, and theological integrity, and honest history.

INDEX

Index